**ART BOOKS**

FROM CRESCENT MOON PUBLISHING

*Leonardo da Vinci*
by James Pearson

*Early Netherlandish Painting*
by Rosalind Mutter

*Piero della Francesca*
by Naomi Haskell

*Giovanni Bellini*
by Julia Davis

*Eric Gill: Nuptials of God*
by Anthony Hoyland

*Minimal Art and Artists In the 1960s and After*
by Laura Garrard

*Postwar Art*
by George Knighton

*Vincent van Gogh: Visionary Landscapes*
by Stuart Morris

*Max Beckmann*
by Stuart Morris

*Egon Schiele: Sex and Death in Purple Stockings*
by D. Simon Eade

*Mark Rothko: The Art of Transcendence*
by Julia Davis

*Jasper Johns*
by L.M. Poole

*Brice Marden*
by Laura Garrard

*Frank Stella: American Abstract Artist*
by James Pearson

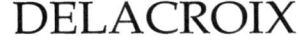

DELACROIX

# DELACROIX

## BY PAUL G. KONODY

CRESCENT MOON

First published 1911. This edition © 2020.

Set in Book Antiqua 10 on 14pt.
Designed by Radiance Graphics.

Thanks to the authors and publishers quoted.

*British Library Cataloguing in Publication data*

*ISBN-13 9781861716661 (Pbk)*
*ISBN-13 9781861717740 (Pbk)*
*ISBN-13 9781861717085 (Hbk)*

*CRESCENT MOON PUBLISHING*
*P.O. Box 1312, Maidstone, Kent, ME14 5XU*
*Great Britain, www.crmoon.com*

# CONTENTS

NOTE ON THE TEXT

The text is from *Delacroix* by Paul G. Konody, published by T.C. & E.C. Jack, London and Frederick A. Stokes, New York, 1911 as part of the Masterpieces In Colour series, edited by T. Leman Hare.

The illustrations discussed in the book are included in the illustrations section, along with many other works.

"Delacroix, lac de sang, hanté de mauvais anges,
Ombragé par un daïs de sapins toujours vert,
Où, sous un ciel chagrin, des fanfares étranges
Passent comme un soupir étouffé de Weber."

–

Charles Baudelaire, *Fleurs du Mal*

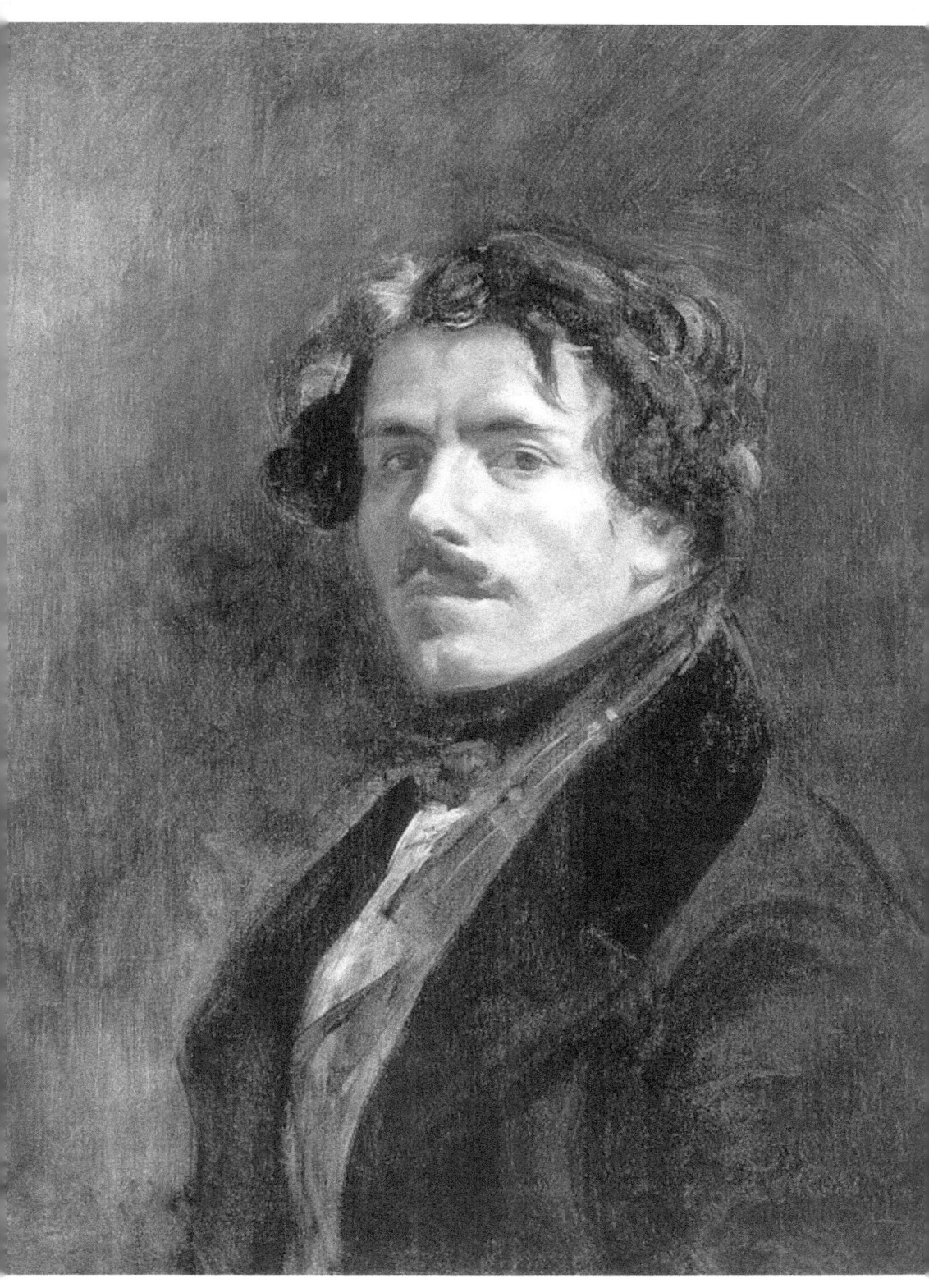

Eugène Delacroix, Self-Portrait, 1837, Louvre, Paris

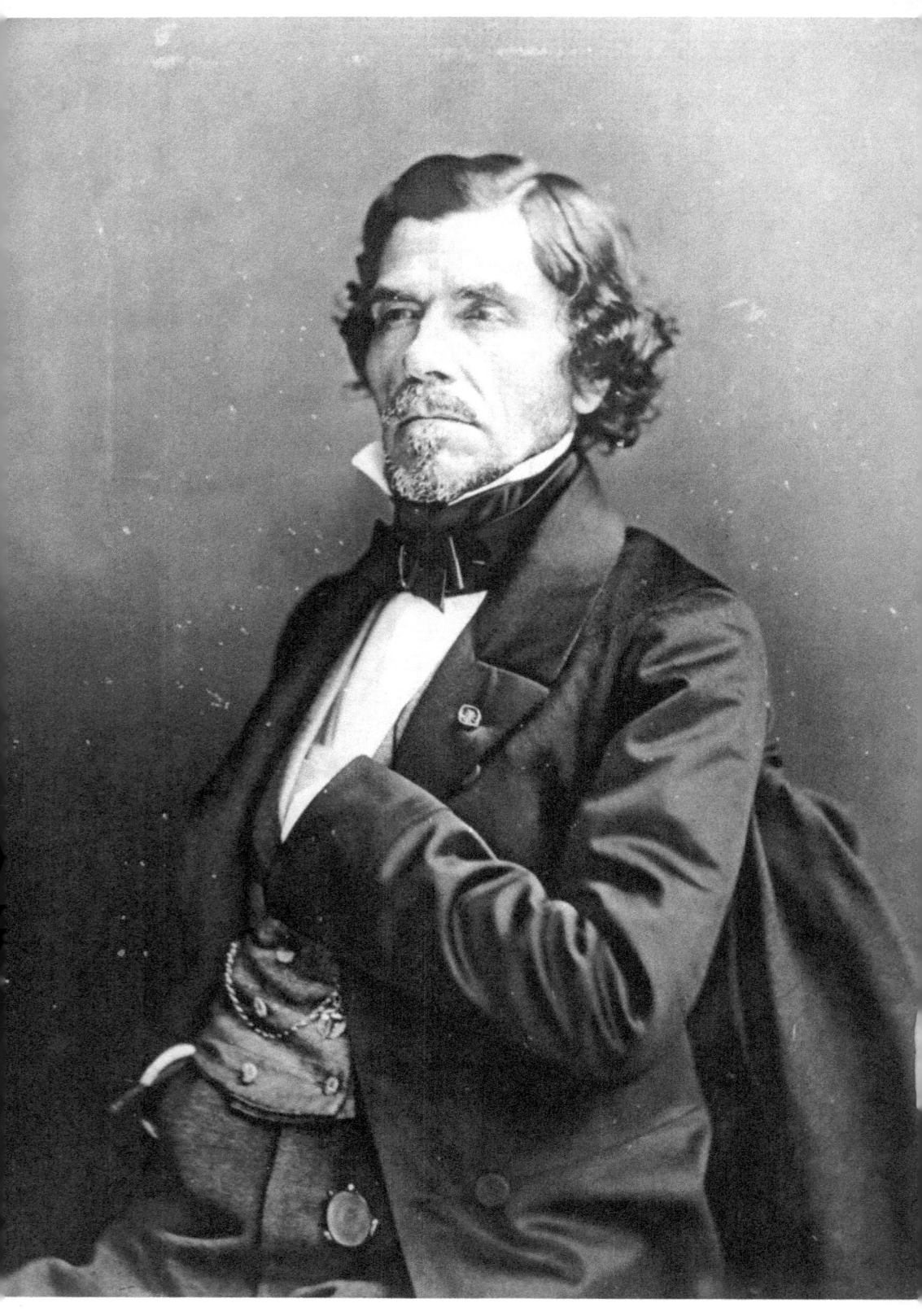

Eugène Delacroix by Félix Nadar

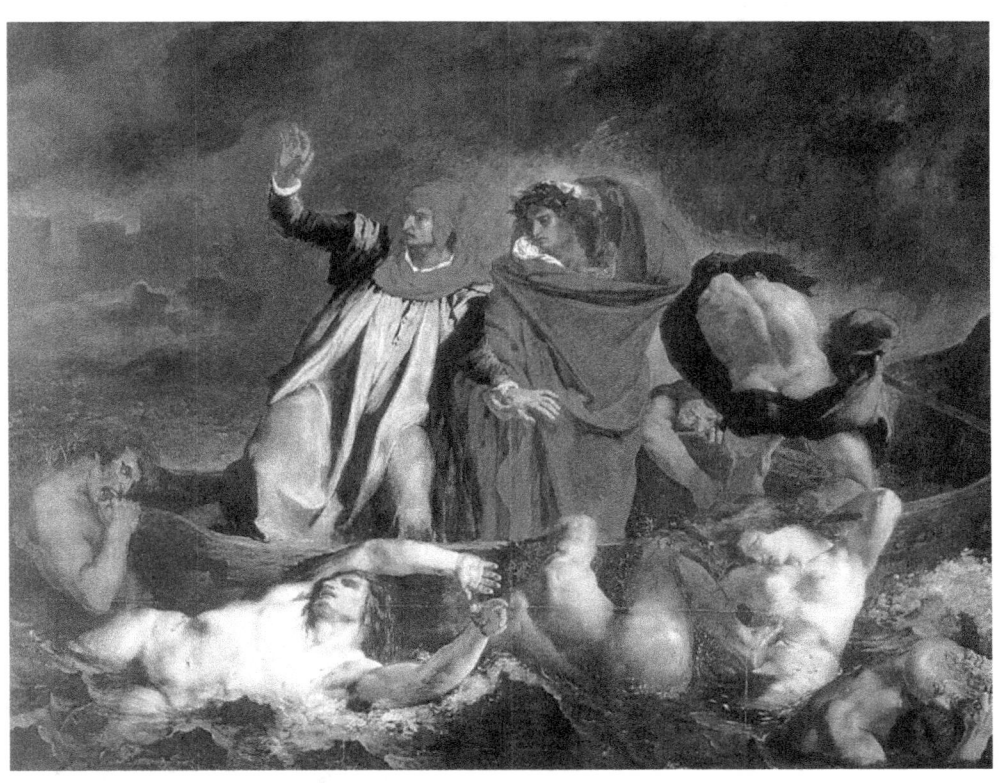

Eugène Delacroix, The Barque of Dante,
1822, Louvre

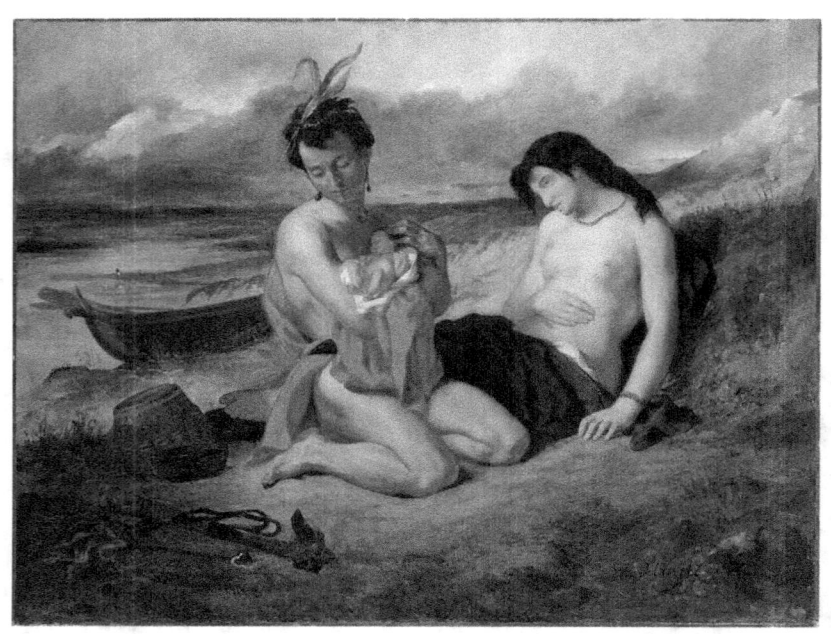

Eugène Delacroix, Les Natchez, 1835, Metropolitan Museum of Art (above).
A Sultan of Morocco, 1862 (below).

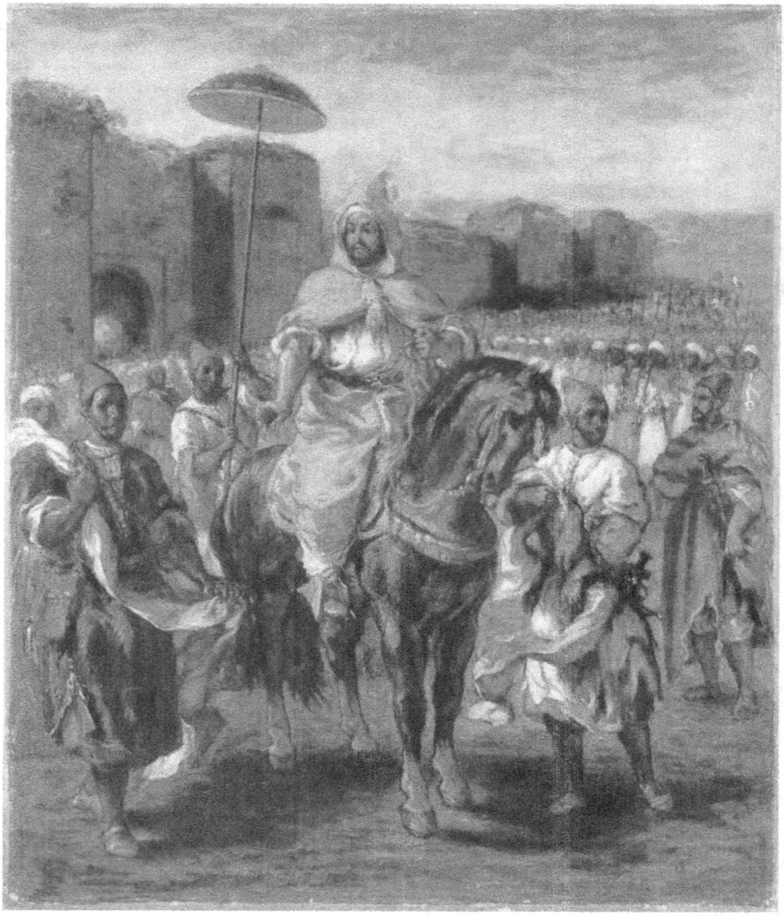

# I

To-day, as one examines the ten masterpieces by Delacroix in the Salle des États at the Louvre – ten pictures which may without fear of contradiction be asserted to form an epitome of the art of the man who is now generally acknowledged to be the fountain-head of all modern art – one can only with difficulty understand the bitter hostility, the fierce passion, aroused by these works when Delacroix's name was the battle-cry of the moderns, when Delacroix was the leader of the numerically small faction which waged heroic war against the inexorable tyrannic rule of academic art. What was once considered extreme and revolutionary, has become what might almost be described as a classic basis of a revaluation of æsthetic values. Even Manet's "Olympia," the starting-point of a more recent artistic upheaval, a picture which on its first appearance at the Paris Salon of 1865 was received with wild howls of execration, now falls into line at the Louvre with the other great masterpieces of painting. It marks a bold step in the evolution of modern art, but it is no longer disconcerting to our eyes. And Delacroix can no longer be denied classic rank. To understand the significance of Delacroix in the art of his country, and the hostility shown to him by officialdom and by the unthinking public almost during the whole course of his life, one has to trace back the art of painting in France to its very birth. It will then be found that the history of this art, from the moment when French painting emerges from the obscurity of the Middle Ages until well into the second half of the nineteenth century, is a history of an almost uninterrupted struggle between North and South.

All the efforts of chauvinistic French critics have failed to establish the existence of an early indigenous school. Nearly all the early painters who are mentioned in contemporary documents were Flemings who had settled in France. Their art is so closely allied to that of the Northern Schools, that it is sometimes impossible to establish the origin of pictures that are traditionally ascribed to French painters. But at the same time, perhaps in the train of the Popes who had transferred their Court to Avignon, Italian art began to invade France from the South. Simone Martini's frescoes in the Papal Palace at Avignon certainly left their mark upon the School that arose in the Provençal city; and gradually traces of Italian influence made themselves felt in an art that remained Northern in its essential features. There is at the National Gallery an early French panel, a "Scene from the Legend of St. Giles" (No. 1419), which clearly shows the harmonious blending of the two currents.

Italianism became paramount in French painting when, in the fourth decade of the sixteenth century, Rosso and Primaticcio followed the call of Francis I. and founded the School of Fontainebleau. From about 1532 right into the nineteenth century, the official art of France, that is to say, the art favoured by the rulers and encouraged by the Academy, was based on the imitation of Raphael and the Italians of the decline – an art that was essentially intellectual, cold, and dominated by drawing and design, not by colour. In the reign of Louis XIV., when Le Brun became the art despot of his country, the foundation of the Academy, and subsequently of the French School at Rome, led to the formulating of definite canons of formal beauty and of the "grand style." Evolution on these lines was impossible. French art was only saved from stagnation by the influence of Northern art, from which it continued to derive its vitality. It was saved by painters who, like Philippe de Champaigne and Watteau, had come from the North, or who, like the brothers Le Nain, Chardin, Boucher, Fragonard, and finally Delacroix, had drawn their inspiration either from the Dutchmen or from Rubens and the Flemings.

During the "grand" century there are only isolated instances of painters who resisted the tyranny of academic rule and the exclusive worship of classic antiquity. But whilst the professional painters meekly submitted to Le Brun's tyranny, the revolt which was to transform the art of painting in France in the eighteenth century was heralded, nay initiated, in the field of polemic literature. A fierce battle was waged between the traditional advocates of the supremacy of line and the champions of colour, or rather of paint that fulfils a more vital function than the colouring of spaces created by linear design. It was the battle of the "Poussinistes" and the "Rubénistes," the two factions deriving their names from the great masters whose art was the supreme embodiment of the two opposed principles: Poussin and Rubens. Félibien was the leader of those who espoused the cause of academic design with superimposed colour as a secondary consideration; and Roger de Piles became the chief defender of colour as a constructive element.

The dawn of the eighteenth century, and the advent of Watteau, brought the signal victory of the Rubénistes. The pompous style of the seventeenth century ebbed away with the life of the *grand monarque*. The new age demanded a new art – the graceful and dainty art of the boudoir. At the very outset, Watteau carried the emotional expressiveness of pigment to a point where it could not be maintained by his followers and imitators. He had never been to Italy; and though he had studied the works of the Venetian colourists, his art was mainly derived from Flemish sources. But the Academy continued to send its most promising pupils to its branch school in Rome, where they were taught to worship at the shrine of Raphael and his followers, and whence they returned to continue the tradition of the School. Thus

Italianism did not die, though it became transformed by the ascendency of the Rubens influence and by the new social conditions. Mythology and allegory continued to rule supreme in the art of Boucher, which is the most typical expression of the French eighteenth century, but they are adapted to the decoration of the boudoir, and colour and brushwork are no longer subordinated to design. Boucher, the most French of all French painters, is inconceivable without two centuries of the Italian tradition of design and without Rubens's example of handling paint. In the art of Fragonard, that great virtuoso of the brush, the influence of Rubens becomes absolutely paramount. Only a few youthful failures recall his study of the Italians.

Fragonard witnessed the end of the *ancien régime* and the great political upheaval of the French Revolution. With the monarchy died the sensuous art of the *fêtes galantes*. The painting that flourished in the Napoleonic era was more formal, cold, and academic than at any previous epoch. David and his followers sought their inspiration in Roman history, and set purity of line and the dogmas of the School higher than ever. Their idealism was of a bombastic, rhetorical order; their painting absolutely uninspired tinting of pseudo-classic designs. At no period had French art sunk to such a level of dulness. The death of David left his great pupil Ingres, the most perfect draughtsman of the nineteenth century, the undisputed leader of the School. But the day of freedom was at hand – and the liberating word was to be pronounced by Delacroix. The seventeenth-century war between the "Poussinistes" and the "Rubénistes" was to be resumed, although the two parties were now re-christened "Classicists" and "Romanticists." But this time the war was one of deeds, and not of words. Ingres was the leader of an army; Delacroix fought almost single-handed. And, for once, victory did not favour the large battalions.

# II

Eugène Delacroix, who was born on the 7th Floréal of the year VI., as the Republican calendar has it, or the 26th April 1798, according to our own reckoning, belonged to a distinguished family. His father, Charles Delacroix, an ardent Republican, who had voted for the death of his king, took a very active part in the political life of his country, and filled successively the posts of Minister for Foreign Affairs, Ambassador to Vienna, Departmental Prefect, and Ambassador to the Batavian Republic. His mother, Victoire, was the daughter of Boulle's pupil, the famous cabinetmaker Oeben, and was connected by family links with the even more illustrious Riesener. His brother, Charles Henri, achieved fame in the Napoleonic campaigns, was created Baron of the Empire in 1810, and became Quartermaster-General in 1815. The military career was also adopted by his other brother Henri, who fell at Friedland in 1807. His sister married Raymond de Verninac, who became Prefect of the Rhône and subsequently Ambassador to the Swiss Republic.

Delacroix was not an infant prodigy. He showed none of that irresistible early impulse towards art which is so often discovered by posthumous biographers of great masters. Indeed, his inclinations tended more towards music; and at one time he thought of adopting a military career. Even when, at the age of seventeen, he left college to enter Guérin's studio, he was by no means determined to devote himself exclusively to painting. There was not much sympathy between master and pupil. The impetuous youth, with his keen sense of the dramatic and romantic, and his passionate love of music, even if his emotionalism was held in check by intellectuality, felt repelled by the icy coldness of the man in whom the teaching of David had stifled any personal talent he may have possessed. And Delacroix soon found that he could learn more from copying Rubens, Raphael, and Titian at the Louvre than from Guerin's dry instruction. Moreover, he had the good fortune of gaining the friendship of his fellow-student, Géricault, who, inspired by a spirit akin to that of Delacroix, had already broken away from the tradition of the School, and who heralded the dawn of a new era with his intensely dramatic and almost revolutionary "Raft of the Medusa." Delacroix himself tells in his Journal that he was so powerfully impressed by the intense realism of his friend's work, that on leaving the studio he ran through the streets like a madman. How much he benefited by Géricault's example became clear when his "Dante and Virgil" appeared at the Salon of 1822, raising its author with a single bound to fame.

Delacroix's mother died in 1819. His small heritage was swallowed up by a lawsuit. His position would have been desperate, but for the help of Géricault, who procured him a commission for an altarpiece for the Convent of the Ladies of the Sacred Heart at Nantes. There is no trace of his later Romanticist fire in this altarpiece, and in the "Vierge des Maisons" for the church of Orcemont, which dates from the same period. Both pictures are based on the study of Raphael. Among Delacroix's intimates of these early days was the English painter, Thales Fielding, from whom he not only acquired his knowledge of the art of water-colour painting – then scarcely practised in France – but who awakened or strengthened in him the taste for English literature and especially for Shakespeare and Byron.

With the "Dante and Virgil" of 1822, Delacroix definitely dissociated himself from the frigid, lifeless tradition of the David

School, of which Ingres was soon to become the acknowledged leader. "That School of Ingres," Delacroix once expressed himself on one of those rare occasions when he broke through his habitual reticence concerning his critical views on his contemporaries, "wants to make painting a dependency of the antiquaries; it is pretentious archæology; these are not pictures." "Cameos are not made," he wrote on another occasion, "to be put into painting; everything ought to keep its proper place."

The "Dante and Virgil" was his first pictorial protest against the rule of cold classicism. To-day we may be surprised that a picture so balanced in design, so sober in colour, so sculpturally plastic in the modelling of the human form, could have been considered in any way revolutionary and should have evoked such violent abuse as was showered upon it by the Davidists. But turn from this "Dante" to David's "Oath of the Horatii" and "Leonidas," which may be taken to typify the artistic standard of the time, and you will grasp the full significance of Delacroix's bold step. True, Géricault had already followed similar aims with his "Raft of the Medusa"; but this astounding picture, a record of a disaster which was then still fresh in the people's memory, was considered rather as a magnificent piece of pictorial journalism than as a work to be judged by the canons of the "grand style."

The case of Delacroix was different. He had dared to bring passion and intense dramatic expressiveness into a subject taken from literature. He had chosen a mediæval poet, instead of going back to classic antiquity. And he had used pigment as it was not used by any of his contemporaries. He had used it in truly painter-like fashion, making the colour itself contribute to the emotional appeal of the drama and giving to the actual brushwork functional value in the building up of form. The writhing bodies of the Damned surrounding the boat and gleaming lividly through the terrible gloom are painted with a superb mastery which recalled to Thiers "the boldness of Michelangelo and the fecundity of Rubens," and which made Gros exclaim, "This is Rubens chastened!"

The outcry raised by the Davidists did not prevent the Government from purchasing the picture for the not very formidable amount of £50. The artist thus honoured and acclaimed a genius by the most competent judges was in the same year placed last among sixty candidates in a competition for one of the School prizes! Henceforth Delacroix abstained from exposing himself to such rebuffs. Even Gros' tempting offer to prepare him at his studio for the coveted Prix de Rome could not shake his determination. He continued to work independently, gaining his bare livelihood by caricatures and lithographic illustrations of no particular distinction. He never went to Italy; and it is worthy of note that herein he followed the rare example of the two greatest *painters* of his country: both Watteau and Chardin had kept clear of Rome and its baneful influence.

The horrors of the Greek War of Independence provided Delacroix with a magnificent subject in the "Massacre of Scio," which he sent to the Salon of 1824. Here was indeed rank defiance of those rules of "the beautiful" in art which had been formulated by the School of David, and which even in a scene of bloodshed and horror expected heroic poses and the theatrical grouping of the "grand style." Delacroix had dared to depict hideous death in the agonised face of the woman with the child on the right of the picture, blank despair verging on insanity in the old woman by her side, the languor of approaching death in the limp form of the man in the centre. He had arranged his composition contrary to all accepted rules; he had painted it with the fire of an inspired colourist. The glitter of light and atmosphere was spread over the receding landscape and sky – Delacroix had seen Constable's "Hay Wain" and two other works by the English master at this very Salon. They came to him as a revelation. He obtained permission to withdraw his picture for a few days, and – so the story goes – completely repainted it with incredible rapidity. The truth is probably that under the impulse of the profound impression created upon him by Constable's art, he added certain touches and extensive glazes to the background. In this connection it is interesting to note that M. Cheramy, whose magnificent collection includes a superbly painted study of the dead mother and child for the "Massacre of Scio," has bequeathed this important fragment to the National Gallery, on condition that it shall hang "beside the best Constable."

The "Massacre of Scio" was violently attacked as an outrage against good taste, but found a warm defender in the Baron Gérard, and was again bought by the Government for £320. It may not be out of place here to state that there is but scant justification for the often-repeated assertion that Delacroix's rare genius did not receive official recognition until very late in the master's life, and that he was not given his fair share of official commissions. We have seen that, in spite of the outcry raised by the academic faction, the Government encouraged the young artist by acquiring the first two pictures exhibited by him at the Salon. At brief intervals he continued to receive important commissions: for the "Death of Charles the Bold," from the Ministry of the Interior; the great battle-piece "Taillebourg," for the gallery at Versailles; the decoration of the Chamber of Deputies, of the Libraries at the Luxembourg and the Palais Bourbon, of the Salon de la Paix at the Hôtel de Ville, of a chapel in the Church of Saint Sulpice; a wall-painting in the Church of St. Denis; the "St. Sebastian" for the Church of Nantua; and the ceiling of the Galerie d'Apollon at the Louvre – not to speak of the numerous works commissioned or bought from him by Louis-Philippe. Thus, it will be seen, there was no lack of "official recognition," although it is quite true that to within a few years of his death he was generally forced to accept wholly inadequate prices for his paintings.

# III

Delacroix's friendship with Thales Fielding and Bonington and his love of English romantic literature had awakened in him the desire to visit London. He undertook the little journey in 1825. He was much impressed by the immensity of London, the "absence of all that we call architecture," the horses and carriages, the river, Richmond, and Greenwich; and, above all, by the English stage. He had occasion to admire the great Kean in some of his Shakespearian impersonations, and Terry as Mephistopheles in an adaptation of "Faust." He was deeply stirred by these productions, which had a by no means beneficial influence upon his art. To his love of the stage may be ascribed the least acceptable characteristics of his minor pictures and lithographs – exaggerated action, stage grouping, and a certain lack of restraint. It is difficult to understand Goethe's highly eulogistic comment upon Delacroix's "Faust" illustrations, unless it was a case of *faute de mieux*, or that he had not seen the complete set. To modern eyes, at any rate, they are the epitome of the master's weaknesses. The drawing is frequently inexcusably bad; the sentiment is carried beyond the merely theatrical to the melodramatic.

Next to the stage, he was interested by the works of the contemporary British artists, with many of whom he entered into personal relations. In his letters he expressed the keenest admiration not only for Bonington (with whom he shared a studio in the following year), Constable, and Turner, whose influence upon the French School he readily admitted, but also for Lawrence – "the flower of politeness and truly a painter of princes … he is inimitable" – and for Wilkie, whose sketches and studies he declared to be beyond praise, although "he spoils regularly all the beautiful things he has done" in the process of finishing the pictures.

Unfortunately the principal work painted by Delacroix in the year after his return from England, the "Justinian Composing the Institutes," for the interior of the Conseil d'État, perished by fire in 1871. The Salon was only reopened, after an interval of two years, in 1827, when Delacroix was represented by no fewer than twelve paintings, including "The Death of Sardanapalus," "Marino Faliero," and "Christ in the Garden of Olives." The extreme daring, the tempestuous passionate disorder of the design of the large "Sardanapalus" alienated from him even the few enlightened spirits who had espoused his cause on the two former occasions. The reception of the picture was disastrous. Delacroix himself admitted that the first sight of his canvas at the exhibition had given him a severe shock. "I hope," he wrote to a friend, "that people won't look at it through my eyes." The picture raised a hurricane of abuse. His own significant dictum that "you should begin with a broom and finish with a needle," was turned against him by a critic who spoke of the work of an "intoxicated broom." Another described him as a "drunken savage," and yet another referred to the picture as the "composition of a sick man in delirium." His other pictures were scarcely noticed, although they included a masterpiece like the "Marino Faliero" (now in the Wallace Collection), which Delacroix himself held to be one of his finest achievements, and which certainly rivals the great Venetians in harmonious sumptuousness of colour. In this picture Delacroix is intensely dramatic without being theatrical. Nothing could be more impressive than the massing of light on the empty marble staircase, the grand figure of the executioner, the statuesque immobility of the nobles assembled at the head of the staircase. The picture was exhibited in London in 1828, when it was warmly eulogised, which is the more remarkable as Delacroix never seemed to appeal strongly to British taste – the scarcity of his works in our public and private collections may be adduced as proof.

It was on the occasion of this 1827 Salon that the terms "Romanticism" and "Romanticists" first came into general use. Their exact definition is not an easy matter. Broadly speaking, the romantic movement in literature, music, and painting signifies the accentuation of human emotions and passions in art, as opposed to the classic ideal of purity of form. Delacroix himself did not wish to be identified with any group or movement, but in the eyes of the public he stood as the leader of the Romanticists in painting, just as Victor Hugo, with whom he had but little sympathy, did in literature.

Delacroix's "Sardanapalus" led to humiliations that he felt more keenly than the abuse showered upon him by the Press. He was sent for by Sosthene de la Rochefoucauld, then Director of the Beaux-Arts, to be advised in all seriousness to study drawing from casts of the antique, and to change his style if he had any aspirations to official encouragement. The threat had no effect upon a man of Delacroix's strength of conviction. He yielded never an inch. He continued to follow the promptings of his artistic conscience which permitted no concessions, no compromise. During the very next year, in spite of De la Rochefoucauld's threat, the State commissioned from him the painting of "The Death of Charles the Bold at the Battle of Nancy" (now at the Nancy Museum). The picture was not finished and exhibited before 1834, when this magnificently conceived scene of wild conflict under a threatening winter sky – so different from the grandiloquous style of the painters of the Napoleonic epopee – met with the usual chorus of disapprobation for being historically incorrect, "as bad as could be in drawing," "incredibly dirty in colour" – the horses bad as regards anatomy, the sky impossible!

Although Delacroix was too completely absorbed in his art,

which – his one great passion – took up his entire life, to take any active part in politics, he was deeply stirred by the events of the July Revolution of 1830. "The 28th July 1830," or "The Barricade," one of the nine works by which he was represented at the Salon of 1831, was an unmistakable confession of his political faith. Here, for once, Delacroix found his moving drama not in romance or in the history of the past, nor in the picturesque East which, owing to its comparative remoteness and inaccessibility at a time that did not enjoy the prosaic advantages of a Cook's Agency, was still invested with the glamour of romance; for once he devoted himself to the reality of contemporary life, even though the daring departure into realism was thinly veiled by the introduction of that rather unfortunate allegorical figure of Liberty with her clumsy draperies and badly painted tricolour flag. The top-hat and frock-coat, hitherto considered incompatible with a grand pictorial conception, enter with triumphant defiance into the painter's art; and they detract nothing from the epic grandeur of this truly historical composition. In many ways "The Barricade" was more daringly unconventional than any of the earlier pictures which had stamped Delacroix as a revolutionary. Yet its success was immediate and final. That the artist was awarded the Cross of the Legion of Honour, was perhaps a recognition of his political sympathies rather than of his artistry. But this time Delacroix found favour with the public and the critics.

At the same Salon was to be seen another of Delacroix's most striking masterpieces, "The Assassination of the Bishop of Liège," for which he had found the subject in Sir Walter Scott's "Quentin Durward," and which was painted for Louis-Philippe, then Duke of Orleans. It is a marvellously vivid realisation of this terrific scene. "Who would ever have thought that one could paint noise and tumult?" wrote Théophile Gautier in his enthusiastic appreciation of this work. "Movement is all very well, but this little canvas howls, yells, and blasphemes!" The realisation of the wild and sanguinary orgy described by Scott is complete and absolute; and yet, in the long list of Delacroix's "illustrative" pictures, there is none that is so strictly pictorial in conception and less tied to the letter of the author's description. It is not so much the detail, the personal action of each participator in the drama, upon which the artist depends to tell this ferocious tale of unbridled passion, but the atmosphere of vague terror, the mysterious gloom of the lofty hall, the flaring flames of the torches, the flashes of brilliant reflections thrown up from the luminous centre provided by the white tablecloth, of the importance of which Delacroix was well aware when he said one evening to his friend Villot: "To-morrow I shall attack that cursed tablecloth which will be my Austerlitz or my Waterloo." It was his Austerlitz.

The Assassination of the Bishop of Liège" was painted in 1829, the same year to which we owe that superbly handled and strangely fascinating auto-portrait of the artist at the Louvre, which he left to his faithful servant, Jenny le Guillou, on condition that she should give it to the Louvre on the day when the Orleans family were to gain once more possession of the throne. This event did not come to pass, but the picture nevertheless reached its final destination by gift of Mme. Durieu in 1872. Delacroix's strangely fascinating personality is completely revealed in this masterpiece of artistic auto-biography. In every feature it recalls that famous description of the master given by Baudelaire in his series of critical essays, "L'Art Romantique":–

"He was all energy, but energy derived from the nerves and the will; for, physically, he was frail and delicate. The tiger, watching its prey, has less light in its eyes and has less impatient quivering in its muscles, than could be perceived in our great painter when with his whole soul he flung himself on an idea or endeavoured to seize a dream. The very physical character of his physiognomy, his Peruvian or Malay complexion; his eyes which were large and black but had narrowed owing to the habit of half closing them when fixing an object, and seemed to test the light; his abundant and glossy hair; his obstinate forehead; his tight-drawn lips to which the perpetual tension of the will had given a cruel expression – in a word, his whole person suggested the thought of an exotic origin."

It is interesting to note how completely this vivid description of the mature man tallies not only with the painted portrait of Delacroix at the age of thirty-one, but with another description of the adolescent, left by his college friend, Philarète Chasle, who speaks of him as "a lad, with olive-hued forehead, flashing eyes, a mobile face with prematurely sunken cheeks, abundant wavy black hair, betraying southern origin."

# IV

The *légion d'honneur* was not the only reward that attended Delacroix's success at the Salon of 1831. He received permission to accompany, at the expense of the Government, Count Mornay's mission to Morocco, which set out in January of the following year. To visit the East had been the dream of Delacroix's life. Its fulfilment marked an important step in the evolution of his art. Now at last he was brought into actual contact with that life and colour of the romantic East which had for so many years been pictured by his vivid imagination. He was away altogether about six months, and much of this time was spent *en route* and in Spain which he visited on his home journey, so that it was obviously impossible for him to undertake any works on an ambitious scale during his sojourn in Africa. But he never interrupted his feverish activity, and brought back with him a whole series of sketch-books filled with pictorial and literary notes to which he had many an occasion to refer when, after his return to the daily routine of his Paris life, he proceeded upon embodying his new experience of brilliant light, sumptuous colour, and picturesque life in a long succession of paintings devoted to Eastern subjects.

Delacroix's Moroccan sketch-books, which are among the treasured possessions of the Louvre, constitute one of the most interesting documents ever left by artist's hand. There is always a peculiar fascination about an artist's self-revelations in moments when his mind is far away from the public to whom he directs his appeal in his finished pictures. And these sketch-books were intended for no eyes but his own. They contain a diary of his progress day by day, vivid impressions of land and people, interspersed with accounts and notes of purchases, and through all the pages run his swiftly sketched, brilliant pictorial notes, set down with the sureness of long experience and practice – sketches of scenery, life, types of natives and animals, architectural details and details of costumes, jotted down with any material that happened to be handy. Some are sketched in pure colour-washes in bold flat masses, some in pencil or pen and ink heightened with strong blobs of water-colour, others in pure outline; and generally they are accompanied by explanatory notes hastily scribbled in pencil. Throughout is to be noted the same swift impulsiveness and definiteness of purpose, the utmost express-iveness obtained by the greatest economy of means. There are some slight thumb-nail sketches – I can recall one in particular of a galloping Bedouin Arab – that verge on the miraculous in the sense of life and movement, the summing up of all the essentials by means of a few strokes of the pen of almost niggardly paucity.

But infinitely more important in its bearing upon his future work than all the tangible yield of this fruitful journey, was the retention by Delacroix's memory of the brilliant colour visions which had met his delighted eyes in the dazzling light of the East. The result was an entirely new conception of chromatic effects and an infinitely more sensuous use of his pigments than is to be found in any of his earlier works. Before his journey to Morocco, Delacroix, though already essentially a colourist in his method if compared with the draughtsmen of the David-Ingres School, paid but little attention to the quality of paint *per se*. Colour served him to enhance the dramatic effectiveness of his compositions, and pigment had assumed a vital function in the building up of forms; but he was still addicted to an excessive use of bituminous browns and warm glazes and paid little or no attention to what the modern studio jargon terms the "preciousness of paint." With the "Algerian Women in their Apartment," which he sent to the Salon of 1834, he entered upon an entirely new phase. It is painted in a rich impasto of luminous colours which sparkle in unbroken strength through an ambient of soft silvery grey atmosphere. The very choice of subject indicates a significant change. In the place of dramatic climax or tempestuous movement and passion and violent emotion, we find here complete repose and the indolent lassitude engendered by the luxurious comfort and by the strong scent of burning spices in the Eastern harem. In a subject of this kind the artist could allow himself to yield completely to the sensuous enjoyment of the rare and at the time entirely novel harmonies of pure, beautiful colour evolved by his brush. The superbly painted negress on the right of the composition undoubtedly owes much to the Spanish masters whom Delacroix must have studied during his brief visit to the Peninsula; and there is as little doubt that she in turn became the progenitor of the wonderful negress in Manet's "Olympia." Indeed, Delacroix at this stage must be considered Manet's precursor and source of inspiration.

The "Algerian Women" was a State commission for which Delacroix was paid the absurdly inadequate sum of £120. His indignation was great when he learnt that a higher value had been put upon a worse than mediocre picture by Decaisne. He almost refused to deliver the picture, but was eventually reconciled by the placing with him of a more important commission, namely, "The Entry of the Crusaders into Constantinople" for the Gallery of Versailles. He was given the commission – but he was at the same time informed that the King wanted a picture which did "not look like a Delacroix"! This picture, which is now at the Louvre, was first shown at the Salon of 1841, and is undoubtedly one of the finest works of the master's maturity. One has only to compare it with "The Massacre of Scio" – in many ways a kindred subject – to realise the master's prodigious advance during the intervening years. The earlier picture, in spite of its undeniably fine qualities, cannot compare with "The Crusaders" as regards subdued splendour of colour. Delacroix himself admitted that the idea of "The Massacre" came to him in front of Gros's "The Plague-stricken at Jaffa." "J'ai mal lavé la palette de Gros," was the wording of his own confession. There is no trace of Gros in the sumptuous scheme of "The Crusaders," and the violent expression of his youthful sense of the dramatic is toned down by a note of sympathetic sadness in the principal figure, accentuated by the unconventional massing of shadow over the group which occupies the centre of the composition.

In the year after his return from Morocco, Delacroix was, largely through the influence of M. Thiers, entrusted with the decoration of the Salon du Roi, at the Palais Bourbon, and thus given the first opportunity for a display of his decorative genius which, whatever has been said to the contrary, was generously acknowledged by his contemporaries, and was given ample scope from 1833 to the time of his death in 1863. But before discussing his architectural decorations it may be as well to sketch in brief outline the course of the remaining years of his life – a life of ceaseless productive energy, interrupted only by spells of illness, but otherwise strangely uneventful. After the references in the preceding pages of the important pictures which constitute, as it were, the landmarks in Delacroix's career, it would be as impossible as it is superfluous to describe, or even to enumerate, the masterpieces produced year by year by his indefatigable brush. A volume of considerable bulk would be needed for a mere list, for, according to Robaut's statement at the beginning of his catalogue: "Eugène Delacroix has left about 9140 works, of which number 853 are paintings, 1525 pastels, water-colours, or wash-drawings, 6629 drawings, 24 engravings, 109 lithographs, and over 60 albums!"

Whether it be due to his unshaken perseverance on the path he had chosen from the very outset, or to the waning interest caused by the wearing off of the novelty, Delacroix's art was now more readily accepted, or, at any rate, discussed without the bitterness of the early attacks. Nevertheless, even now, and indeed to the end of his life, he could only obtain wretched prices for his pictures, and the Academy remained implacably hostile, until the special collection of his principal works at the International Exhibition of 1855 brought him at last that general public applause that had till then been denied to him. Delacroix himself showed no bitterness to the Academy, and presented himself time after time for election, his claims being invariably couched in terms as modest as they were dignified. His first attempt was in 1837, when the votes were cast in favour of Schnetz. Two vacancies occurred in 1838, and on both occasions Delacroix knocked at the doors of the Academy, but Langlois and Couder were preferred to him. His next attempt was in 1849, when Cogniet secured the majority of votes. When he presented himself again in 1853, insult was added to injury, his very candidature being refused! Time has avenged the wrong; the names of Schnetz, Langlois, Couder, and Cogniet are all but forgotten, whilst Delacroix has become immortal.

Encouraged by his triumph at the Universal Exposition of 1855, Delacroix presented himself for the sixth time when the next vacancy arose in 1857, and this time his perseverance at last found its reward – he was elected just before he entered upon the seventh decade of his life. But even now he was denied peaceful enjoyment of his tardy success. His next contributions to the Salon, in 1859, led to a renewed outburst of vituperative criticism and abuse, and this time Delacroix was hurt to the quick. He decided not to expose himself in future to the gibes of his detractors, and for the remaining four years of his life, although continuing his artistic activity to the very end, refrained from contributing to public exhibitions.

The years 1837-1841 mark a fruitful epoch in Delacroix's career. The masterpieces that issued from his studio in these years would alone have sufficed to establish his lasting fame. In 1837 he painted the magnificent "Battle of Taillebourg," which is the glory of the gallery of battle pictures at Versailles, but found so little favour with the jury of the Salon that it narrowly escaped being rejected. The tumult and confusion of hand-to-hand fighting had never before been rendered with such force and such absence of heroic attitudinising. To the next year we owe "The Enraged Medea," of the Lille Museum, and that extraordinary scene of fitful, jerky, furious movement known as "Les Convulsionnaires de Tanger," which, after having twice changed hands at public auction during the artist's lifetime, for £87 in 1852 and for £1160 in 1858, rose to £1940 at a sale held in 1869, and finally found a purchaser for £3800 in 1881.

The "Jewish Wedding in Morocco," in which the painter's concern with true tone-values and beautiful quality of pigment is carried even further than in the "Algerian Women," and the intensely dramatic "Hamlet and the Gravediggers" – both are now at the Louvre – were his chief works in 1839; whilst in the following year he devoted his energies to the large "Justice of Trajan" (now extensively restored) at the Rouen Gallery, and the powerful "Shipwreck of Don Juan," surely one of the most tragic and impressive pictures ever conceived by human genius. It bears the same relation to the "Dante and Virgil" that "The Crusaders" bears to "The Massacre of Scio." And it is one of the most striking instances of Delacroix's power to make colour itself expressive of the mood of the drama. The conception, though based on Byron's poem, owes little to the literary foundation – that is to say, it is not illustrative in the sense that acquaintance with the poem is essential for its appreciation. It is just a vivid realisation of the combined horrors of shipwreck and starvation in which the tragic aspect of sea and sky is as significant as the ghastliness of the wretches whom hunger has turned into cannibals. The sombre tonality and the flashes of livid light, recall El Greco in his later period. To the year 1841 belongs "The Entry of the Crusaders into Constantinople," of which mention has already been made.

At the Salon of 1845 appeared the large painting of "The Sultan of Morocco surrounded by his Guard," which was bought by the State for the Toulouse Gallery at the price of £160. Baudelaire, ever an ardent admirer of Delacroix, draws attention to the peculiar quality of the colour harmony in this picture which, "notwithstanding the splendour of the tones, is grey, grey like Nature, grey like the atmosphere of a summer day, when the sunlight spreads like a twilight of vibrating dust upon every object." "The Sultan of Morocco" was one of the last large canvases produced by the master, whose best energies were now absorbed by his gigantic decorative tasks, although he continued to paint an endless succession of easel pictures, many of which were variations of earlier compositions.

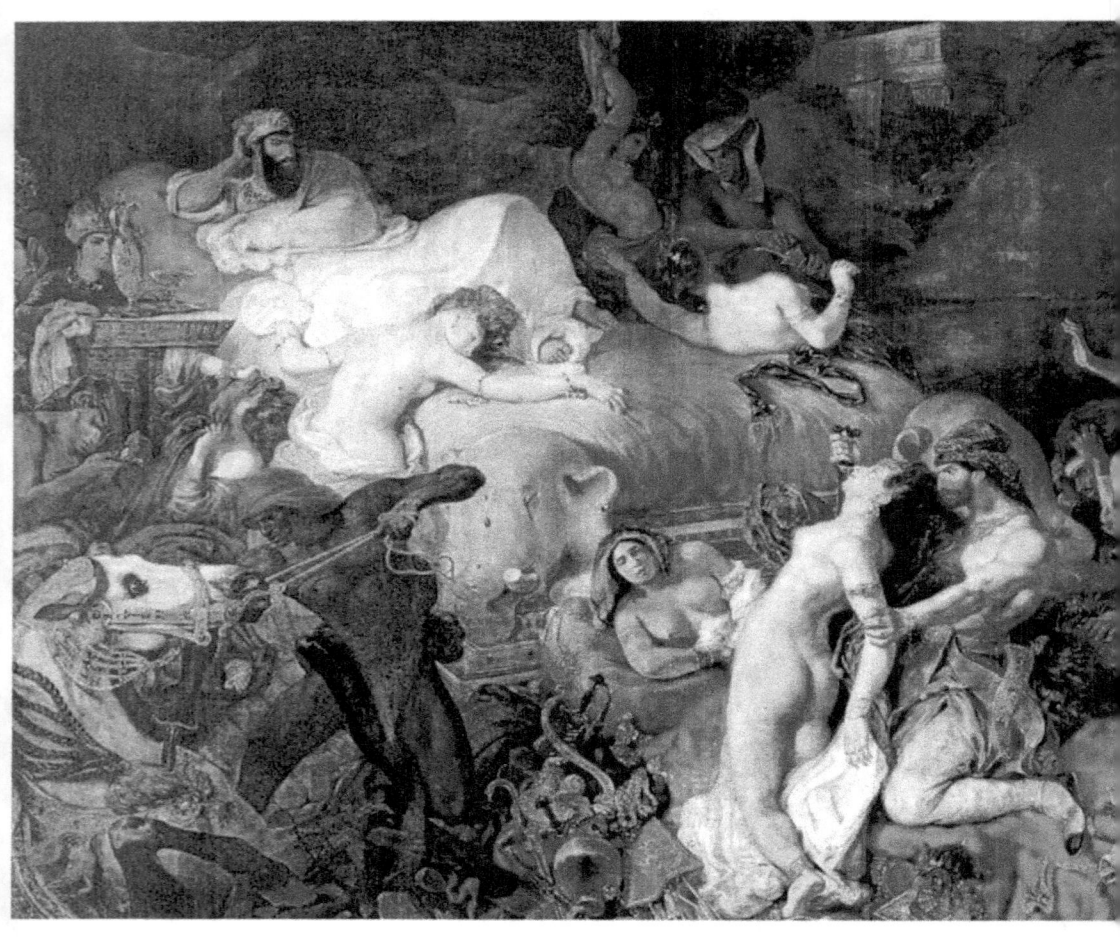

Eugène Delacroix, The Death of Sardanapalus, 1827
(this page and over).

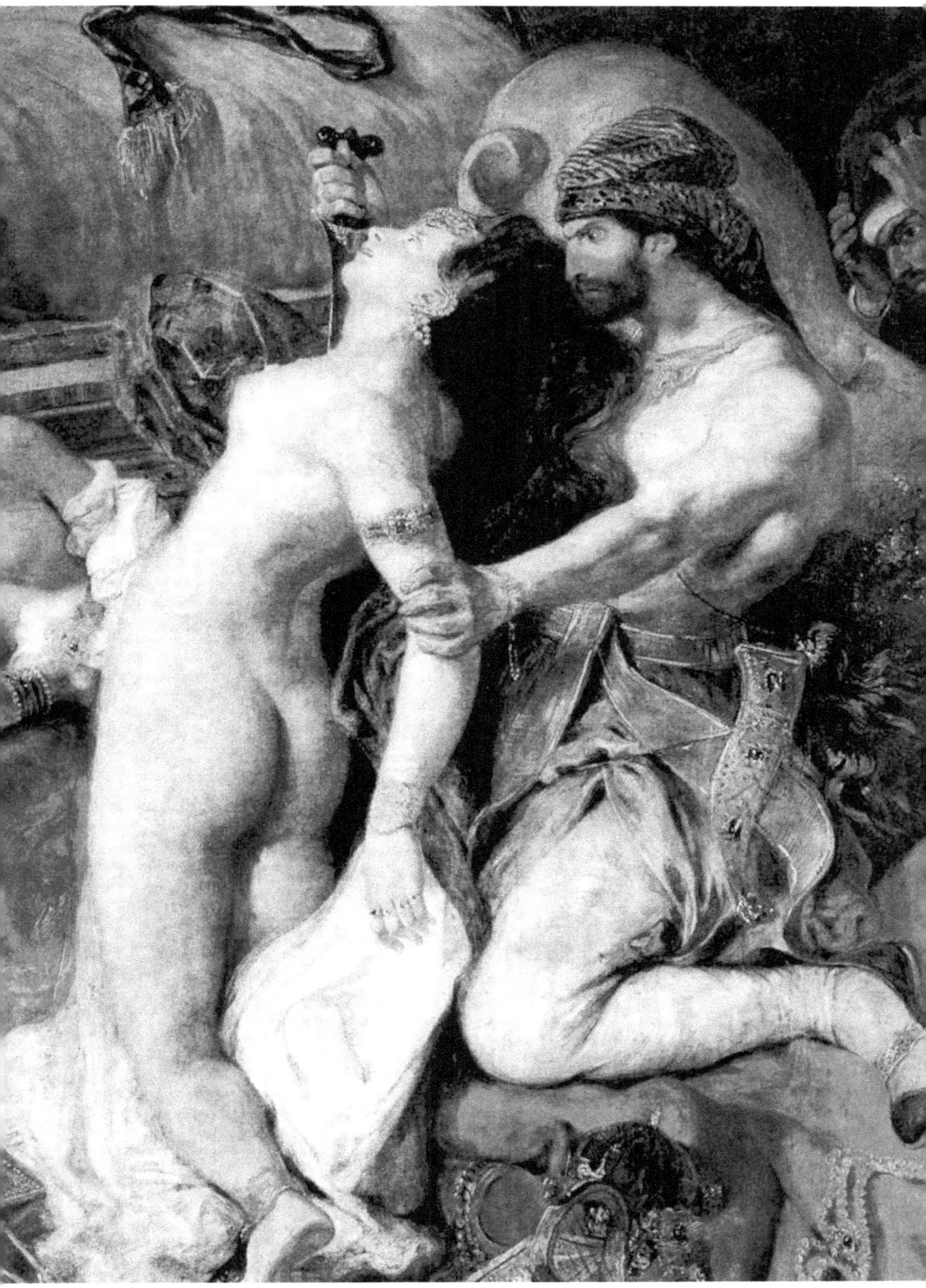

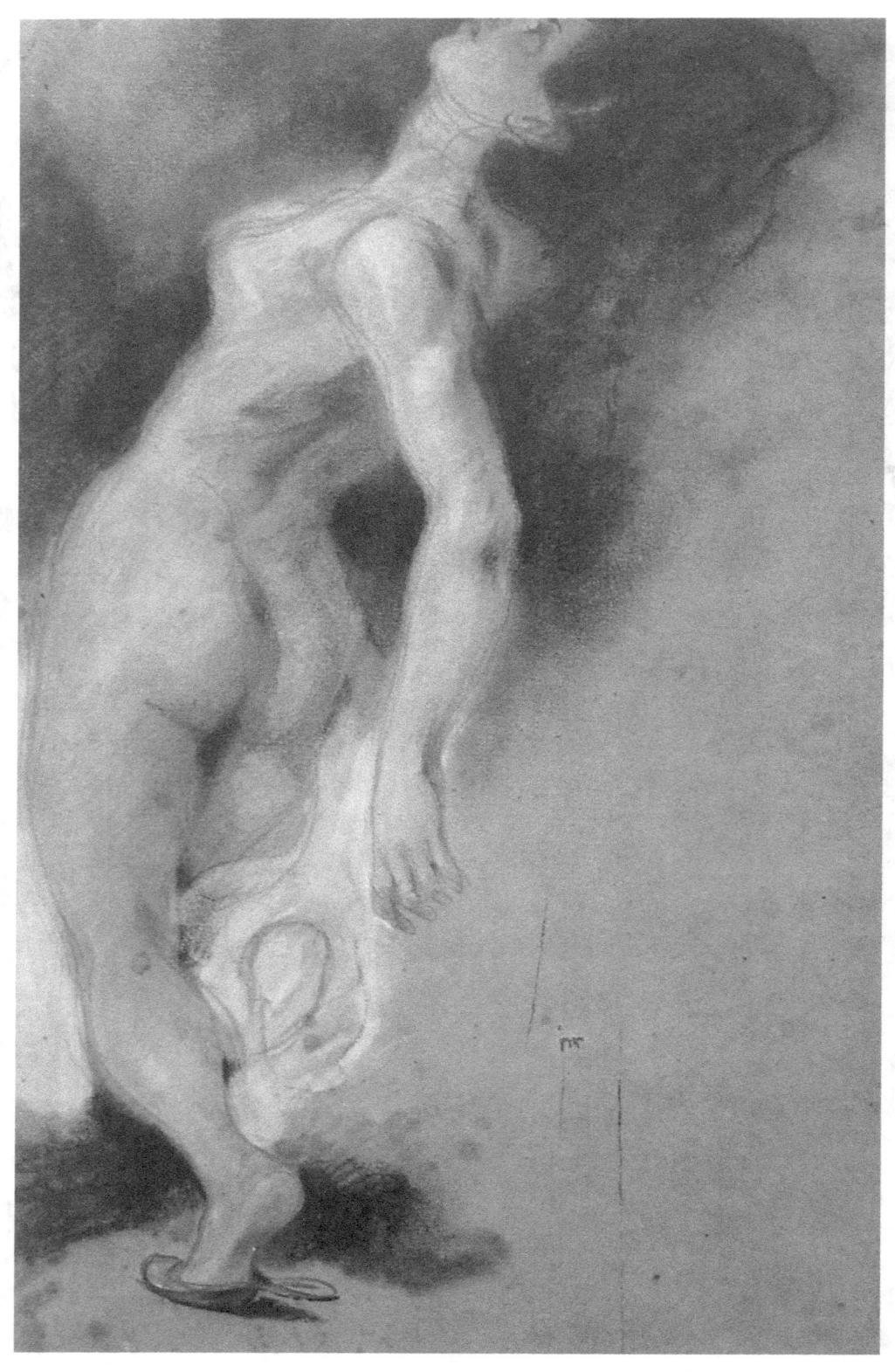

Eugène Delacroix, Study, 1827,

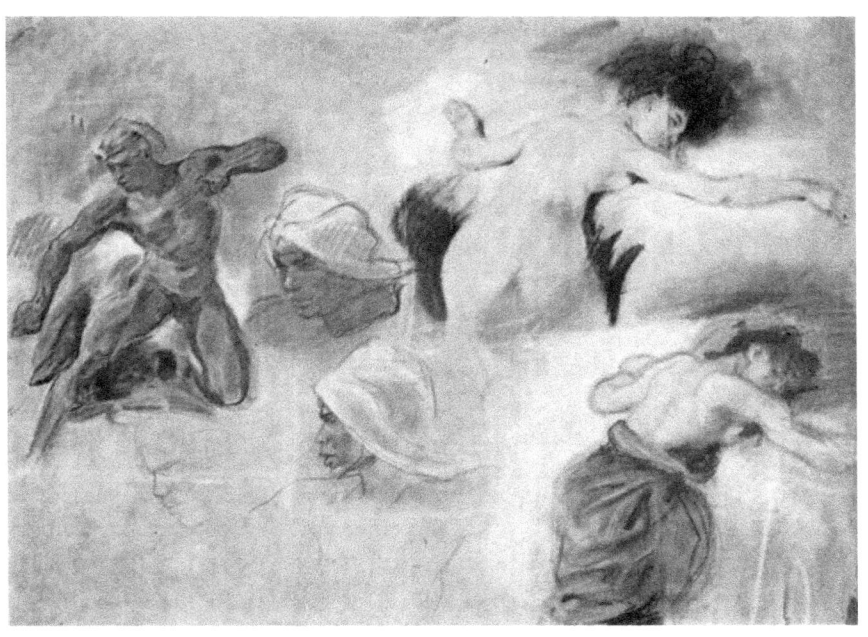

Eugène Delacroix, Studies for Sardanapalus, Louvre, Paris

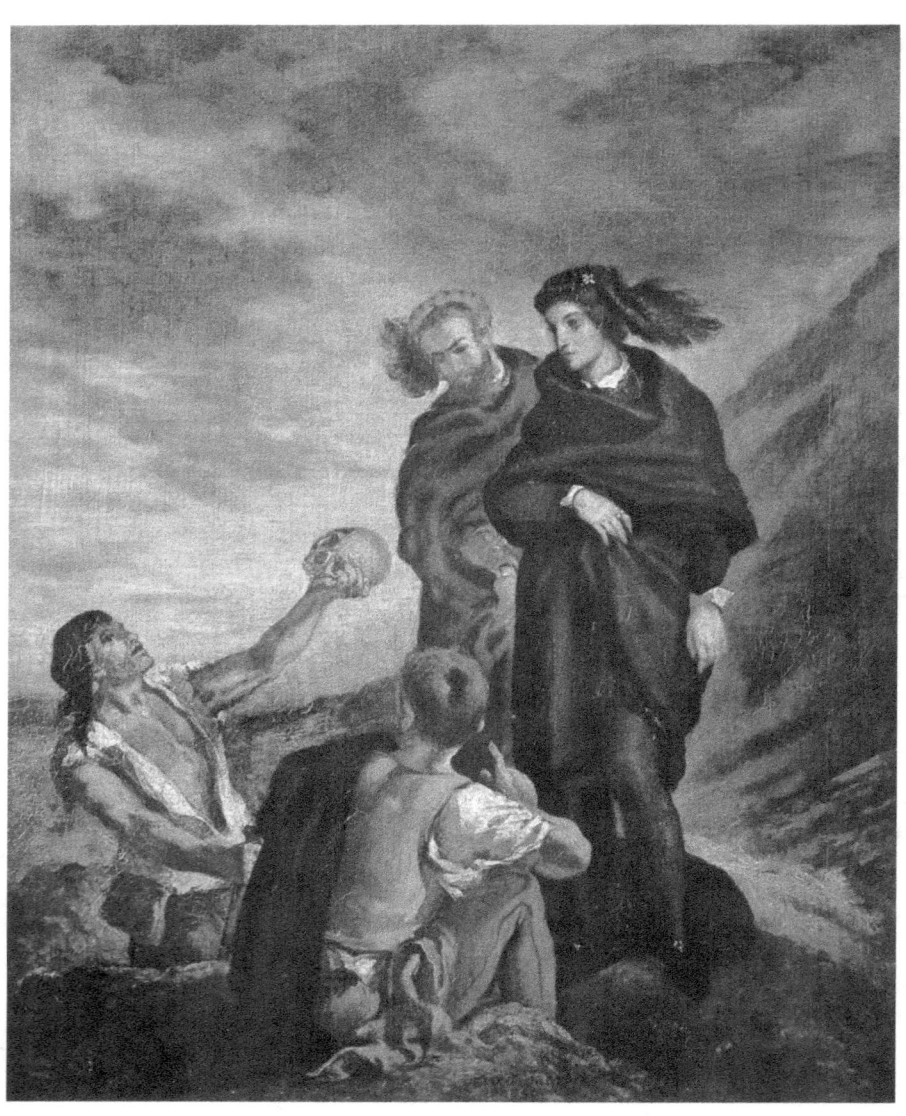

Eugène Delacroix, Hamlet and Horatio, 1839

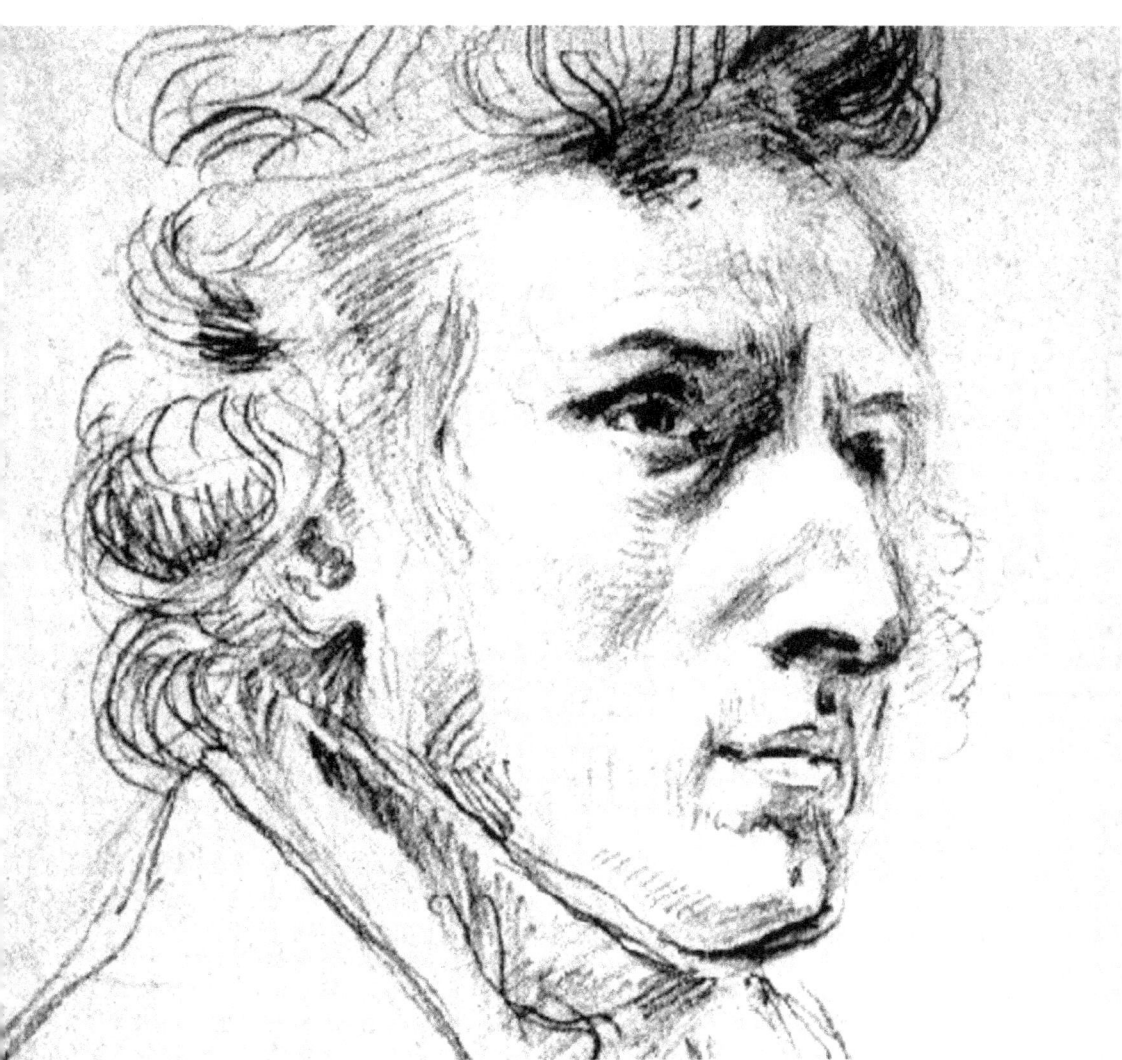

Eugene Delacroix, study for Frédéric Chopin

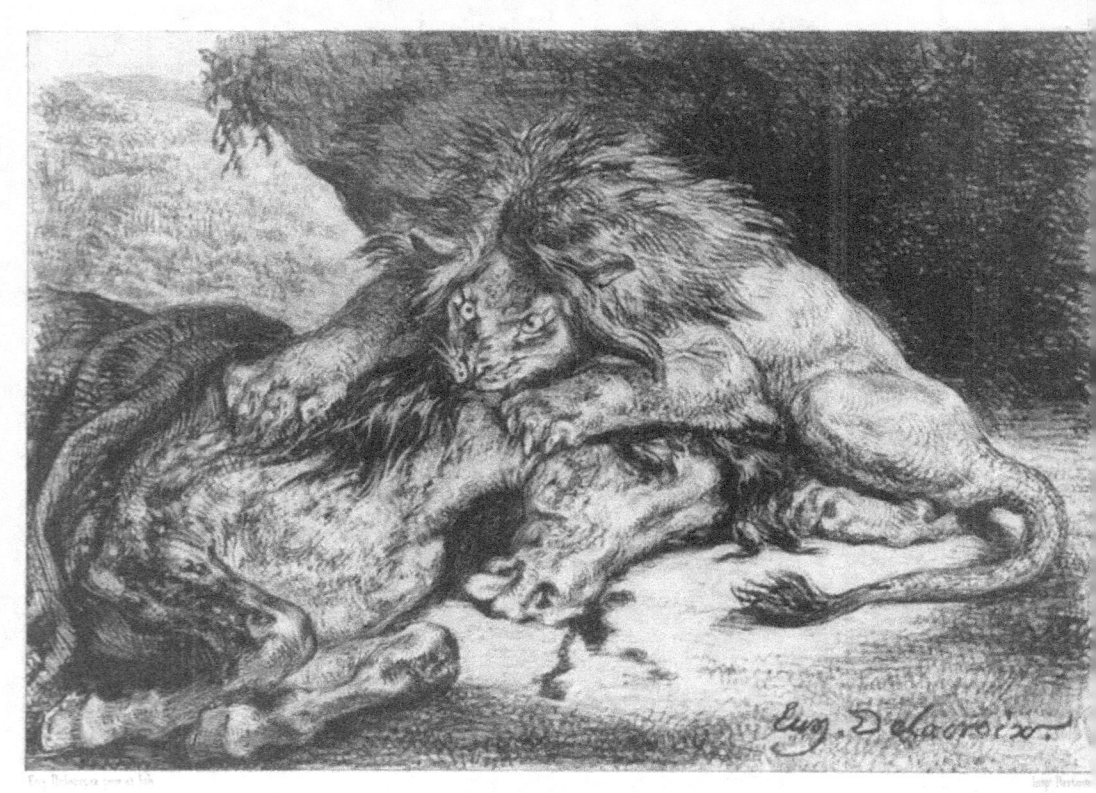

Eugène Delacroix, Lion Devouring a Horse, 1844, lithograph

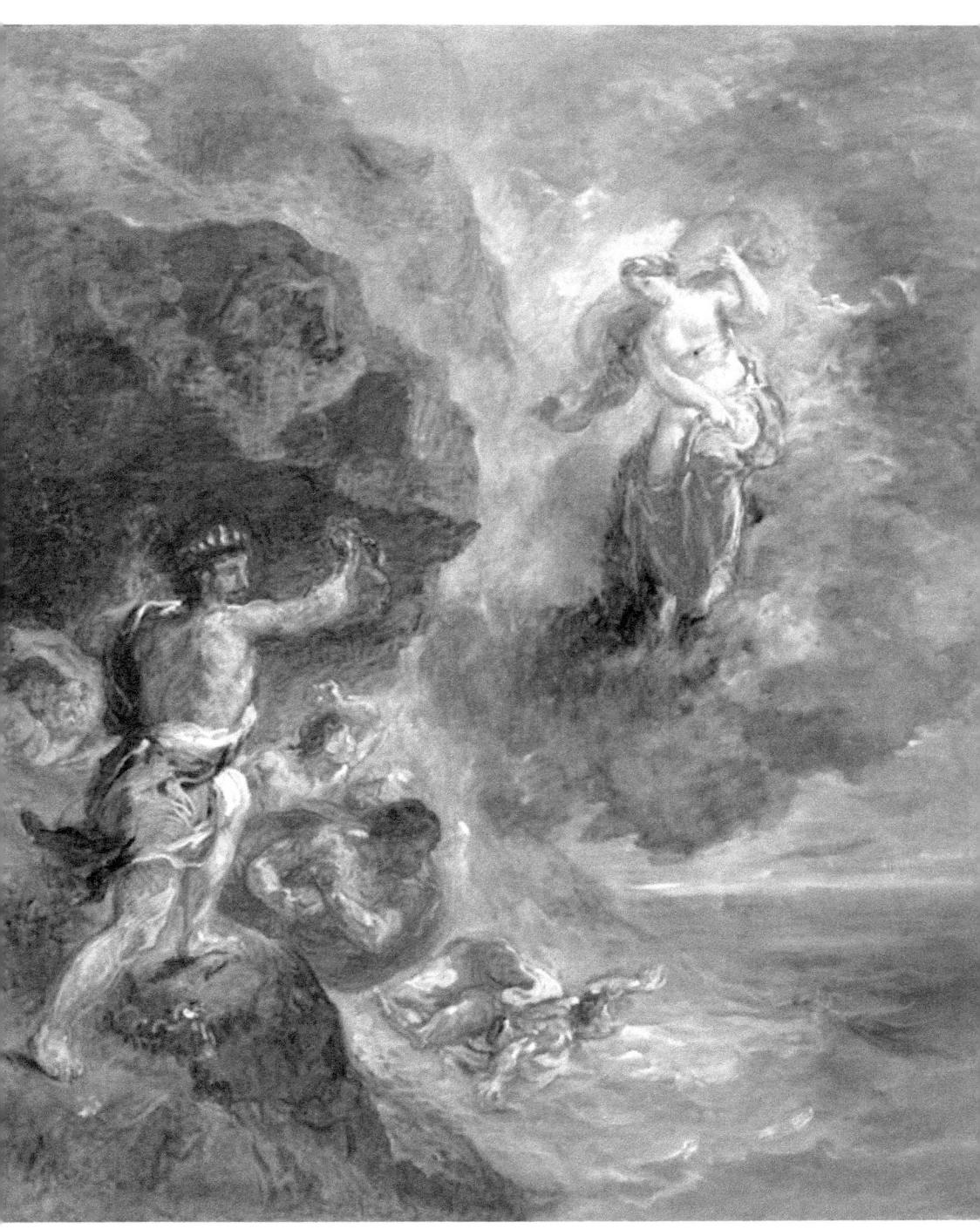

Eugène Delacroix, Winter, Sao Paolo

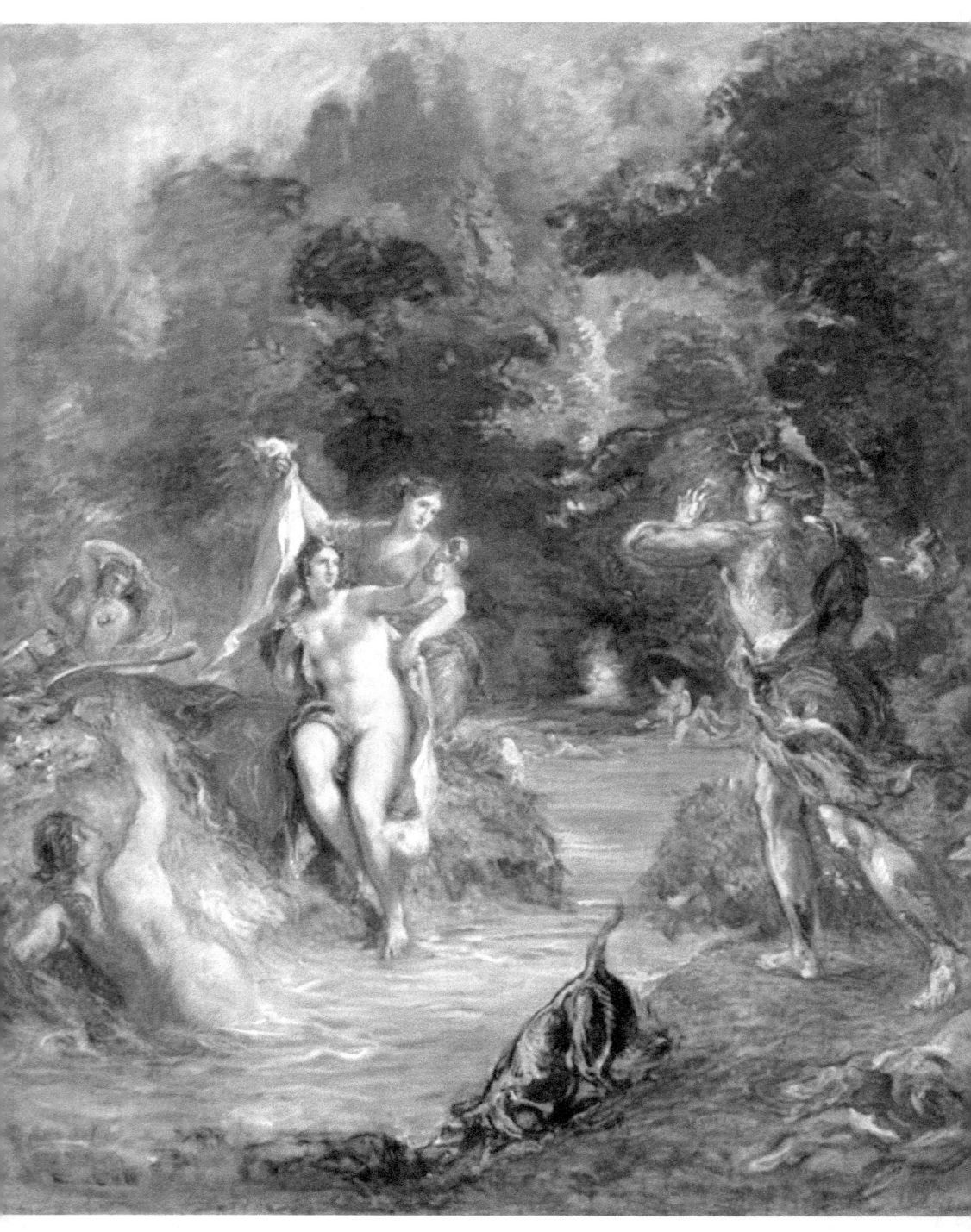

Eugène Delacroix, O Verao Summer, 1856-63, Sao Paolo

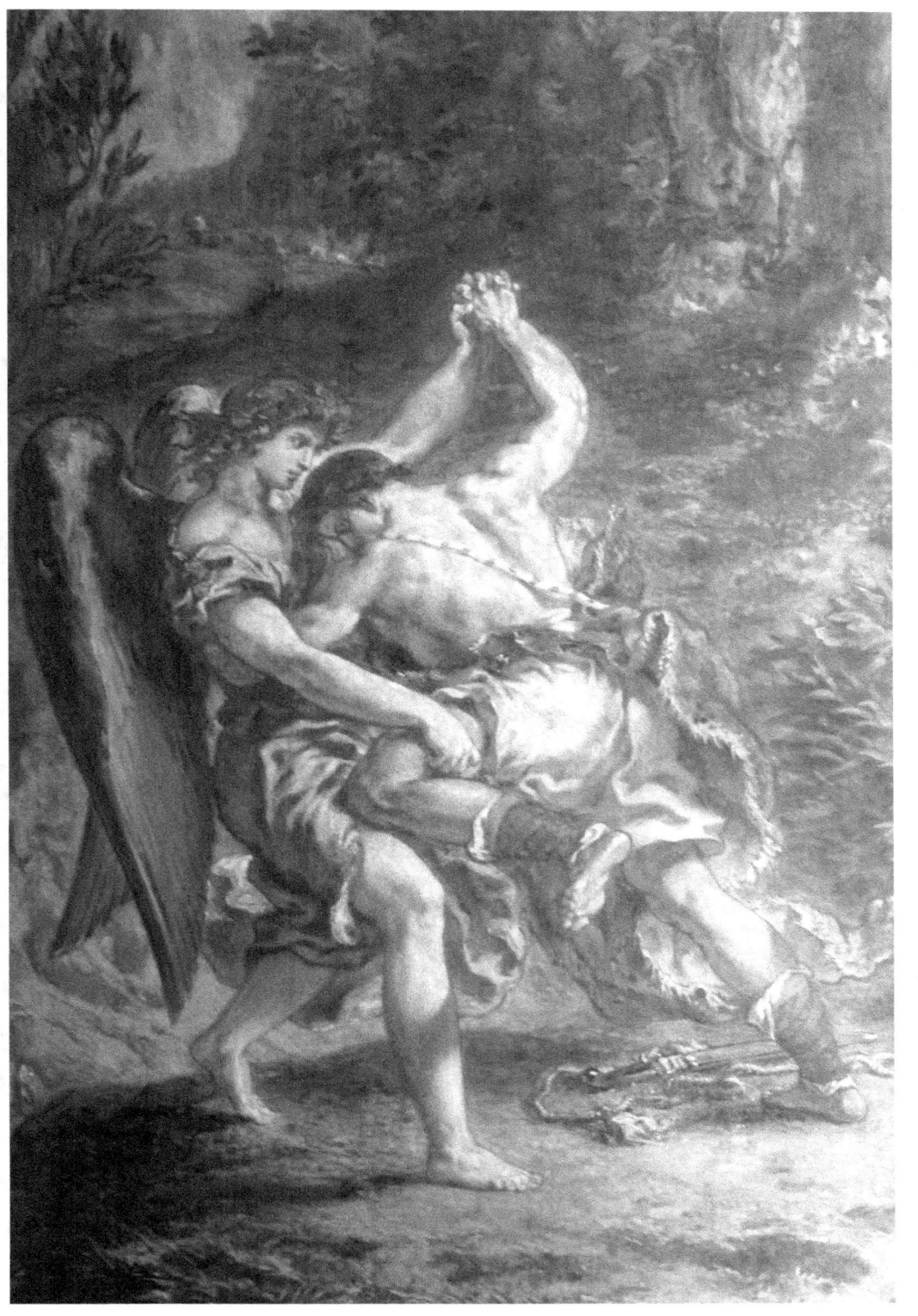

Eugène Delacroix, Lutte de Jacob ave l'Ange, St Sulpice Church, Paris

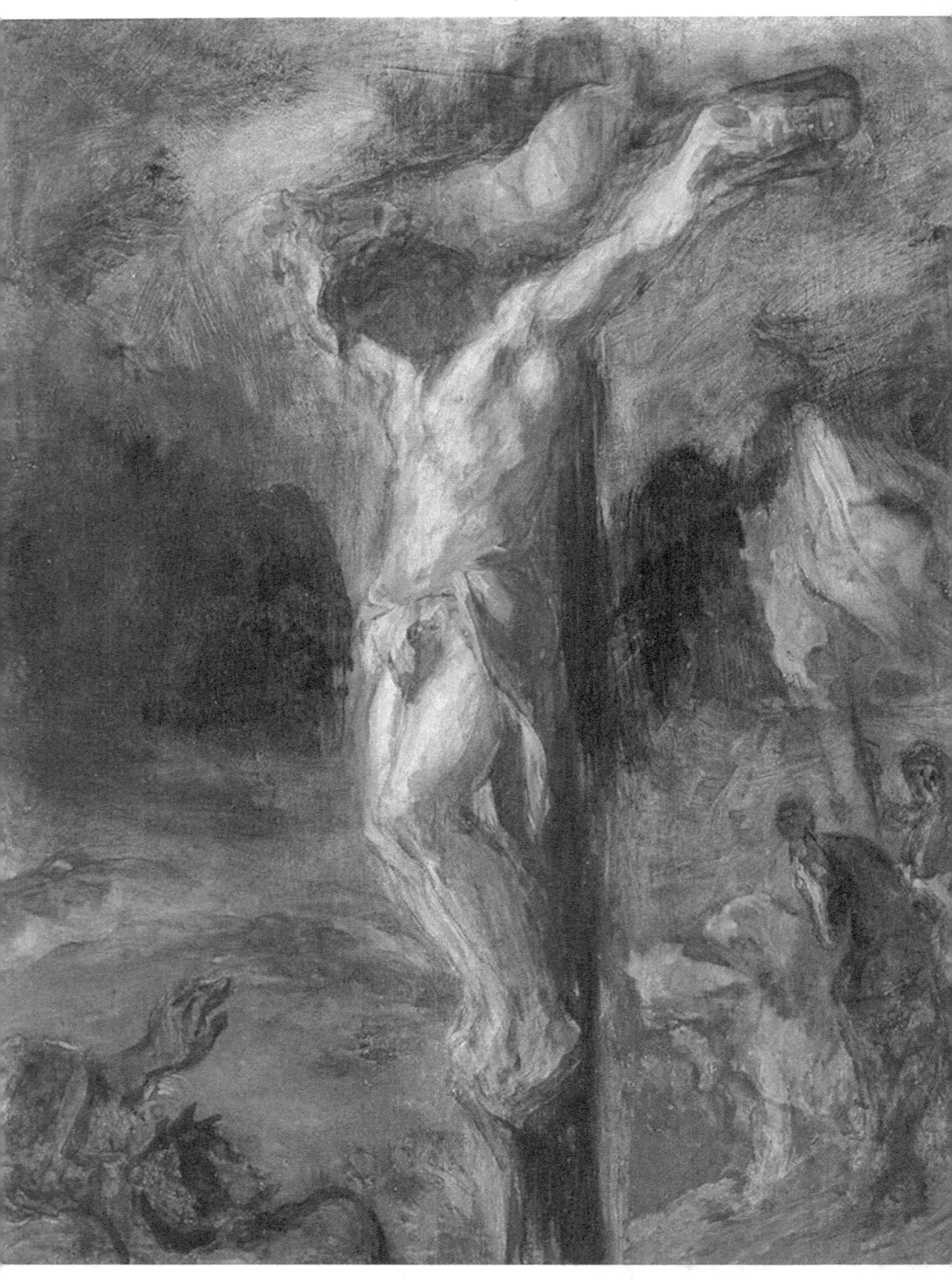

Eugène Delacroix, Christ On the Cross (sketch), 1845, Rotterdam

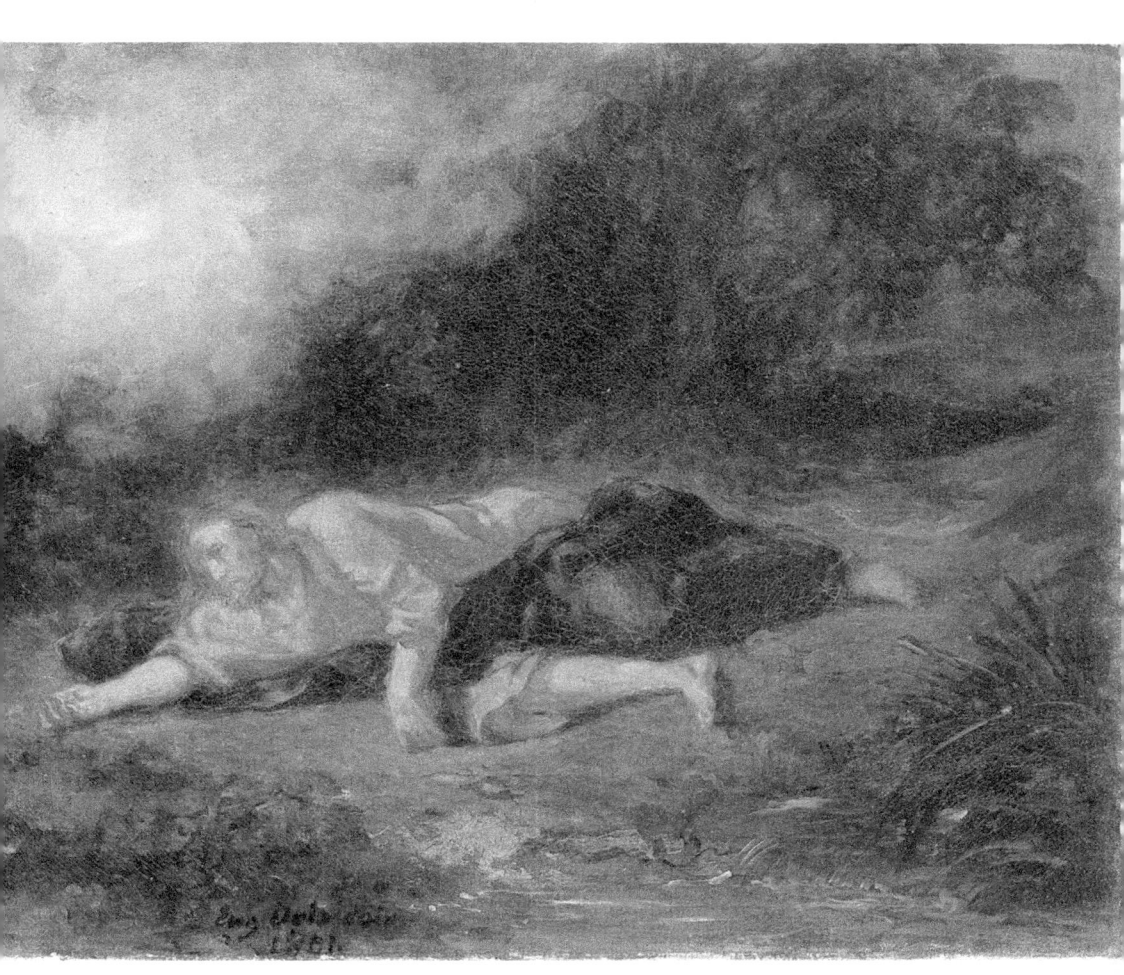

Eugène Delacroix, The Agony In the Garden, 1861,
Rijksmusemm, Amsterdam

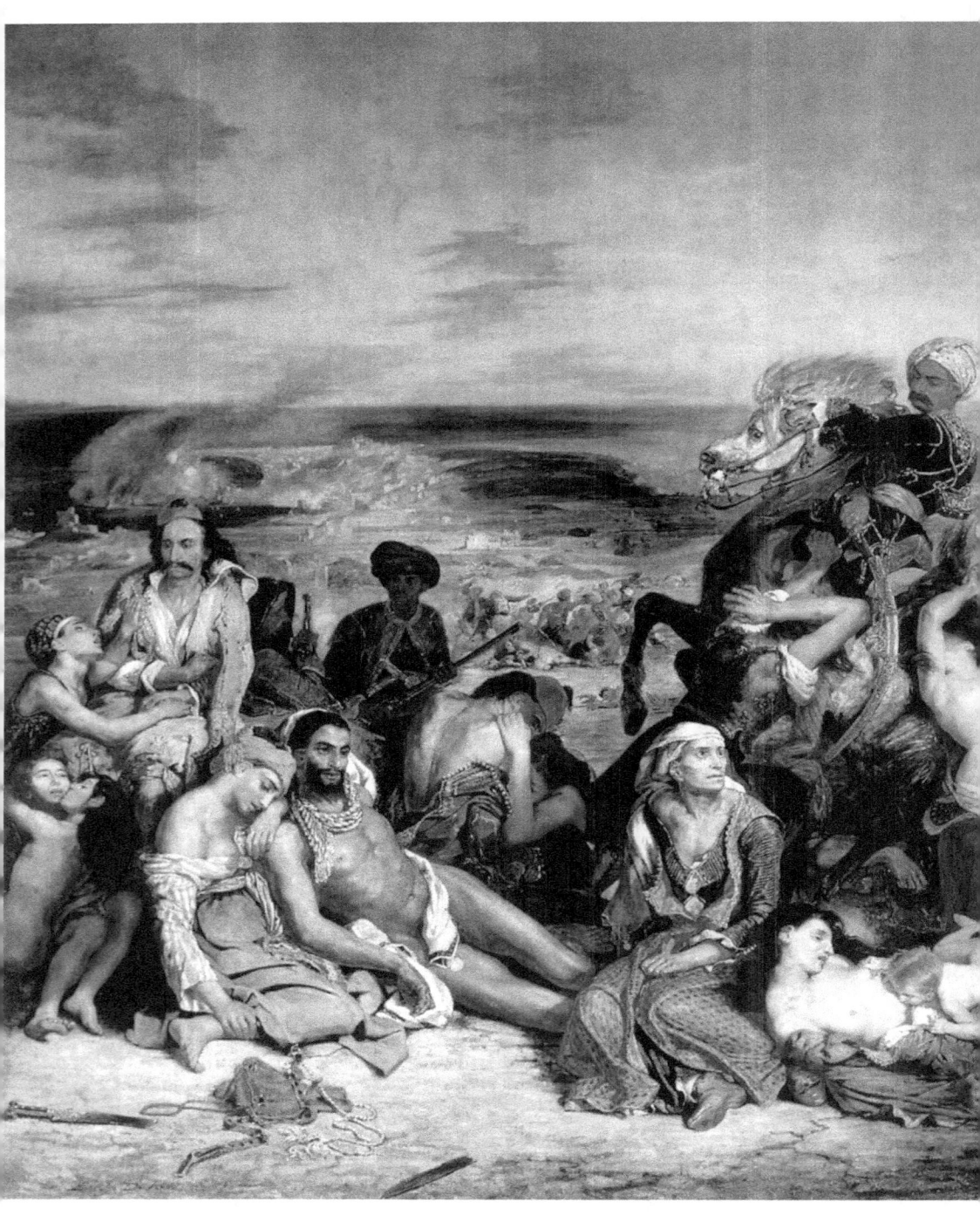

Eugène Delacroix, Le Massacre de Scio, 1824, Louvre, Paris

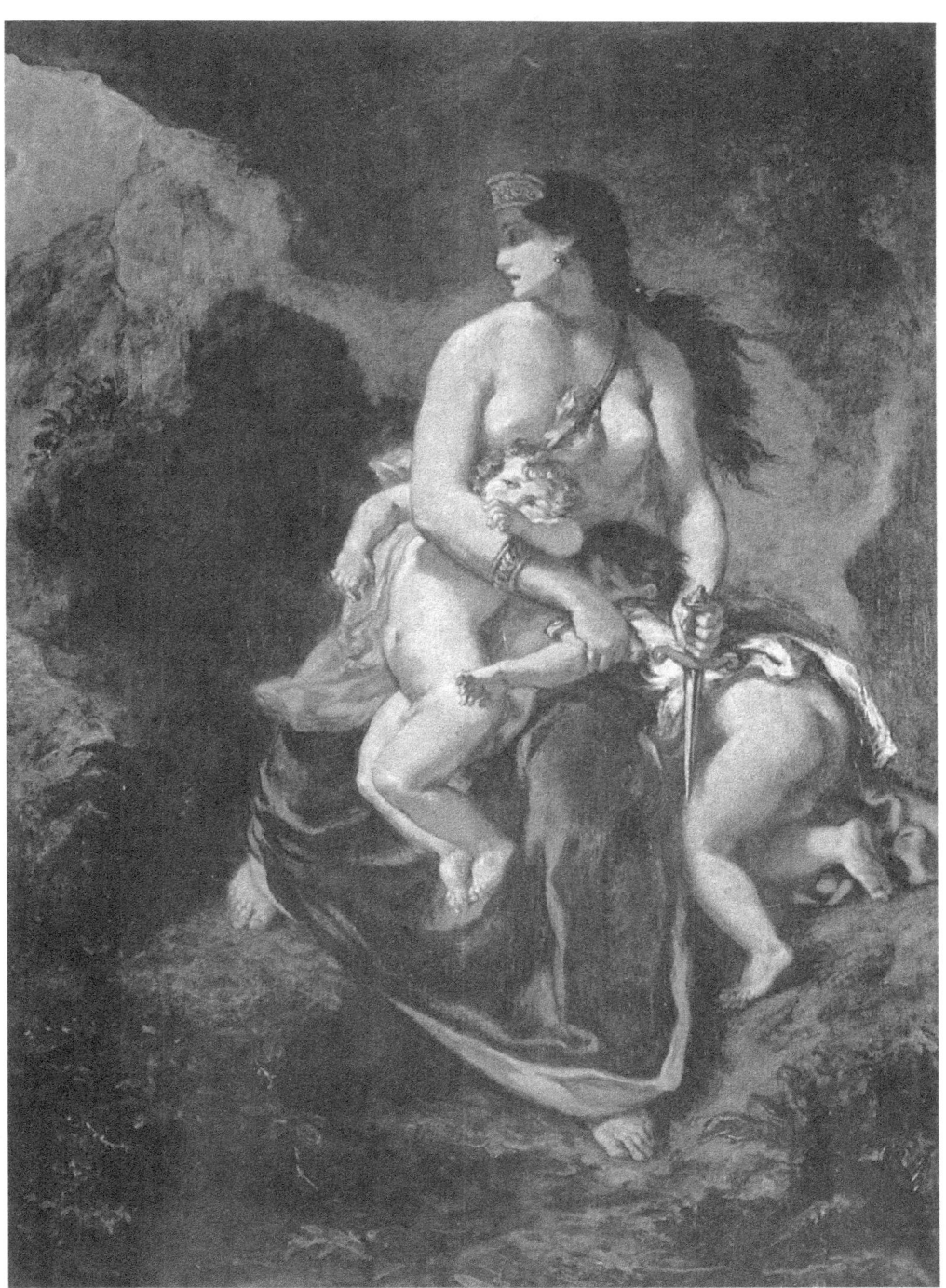

Eugène Delacroix, Medea, 1862

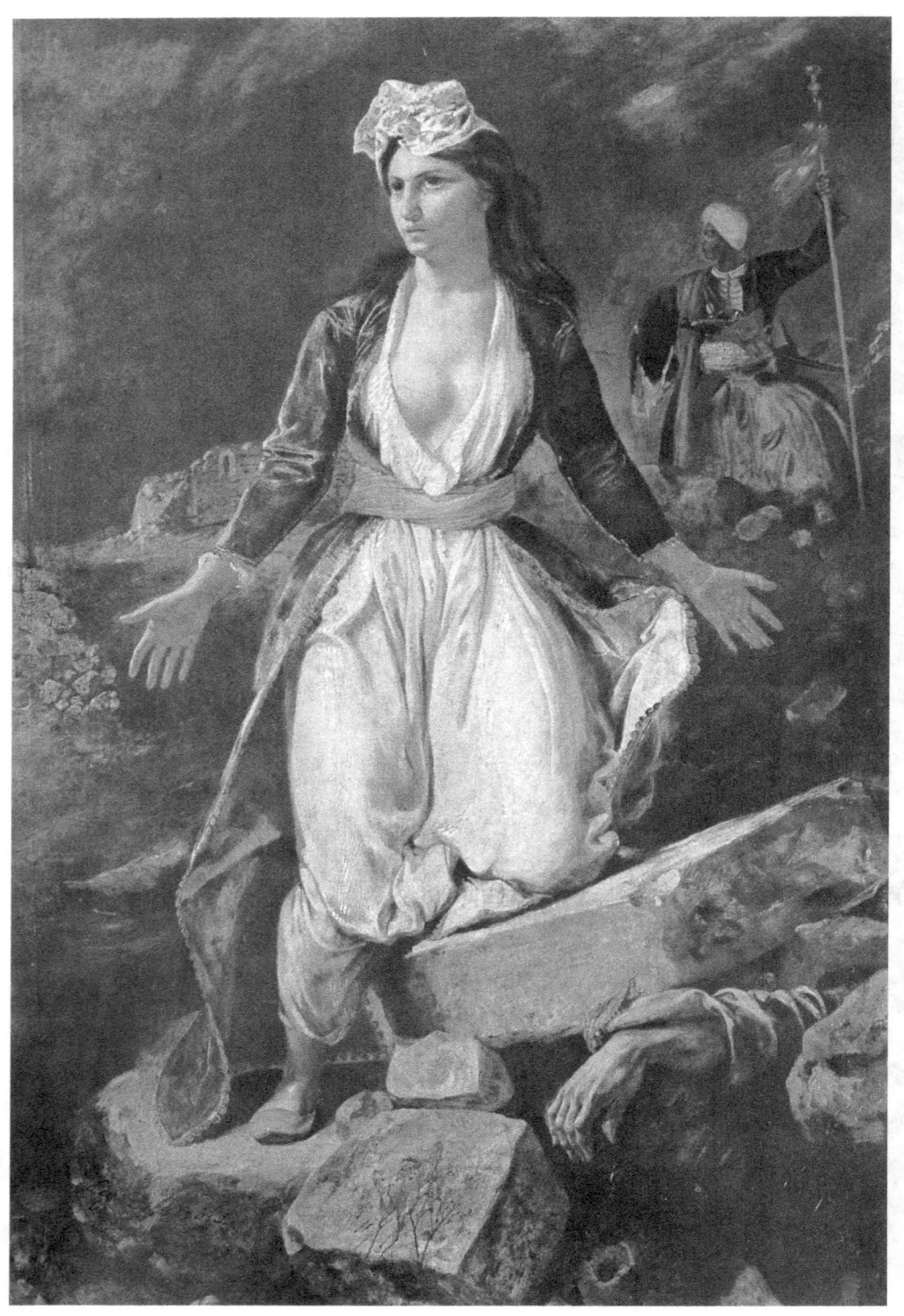

Eugène Delacroix, Greece, 1820, Bordeaux

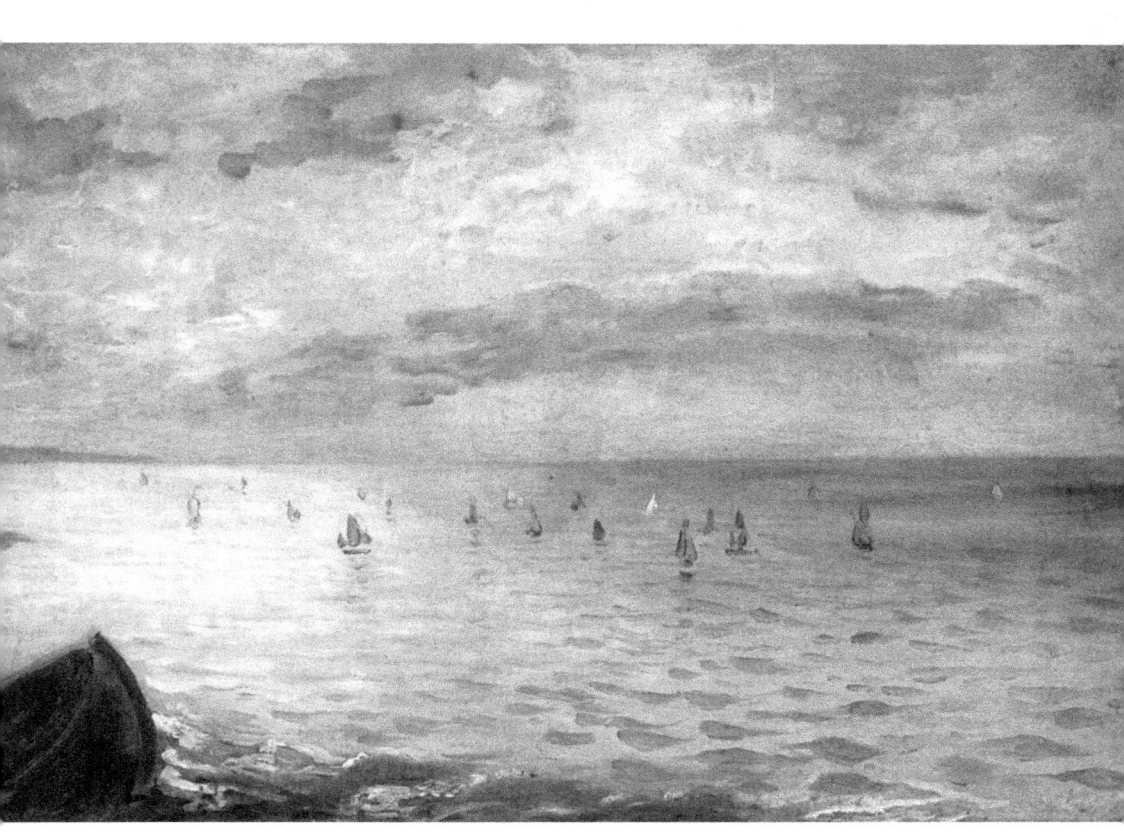

Eugène Delacroix, The Sea From the Heights of Dieppe, 1852, Louvre, Paris

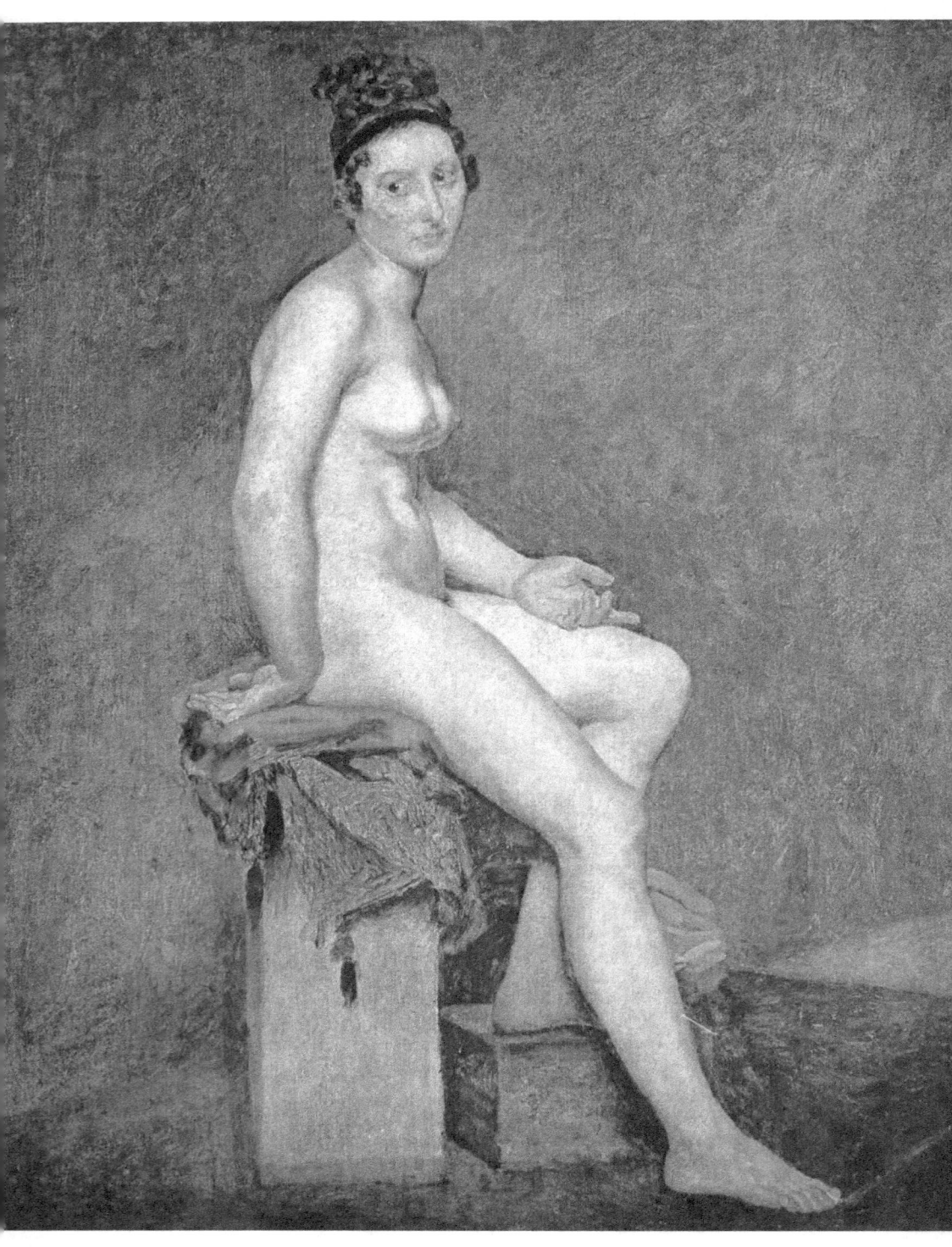

Eugène Delacroix, Nude Study, 1817-24, Louvre, Paris

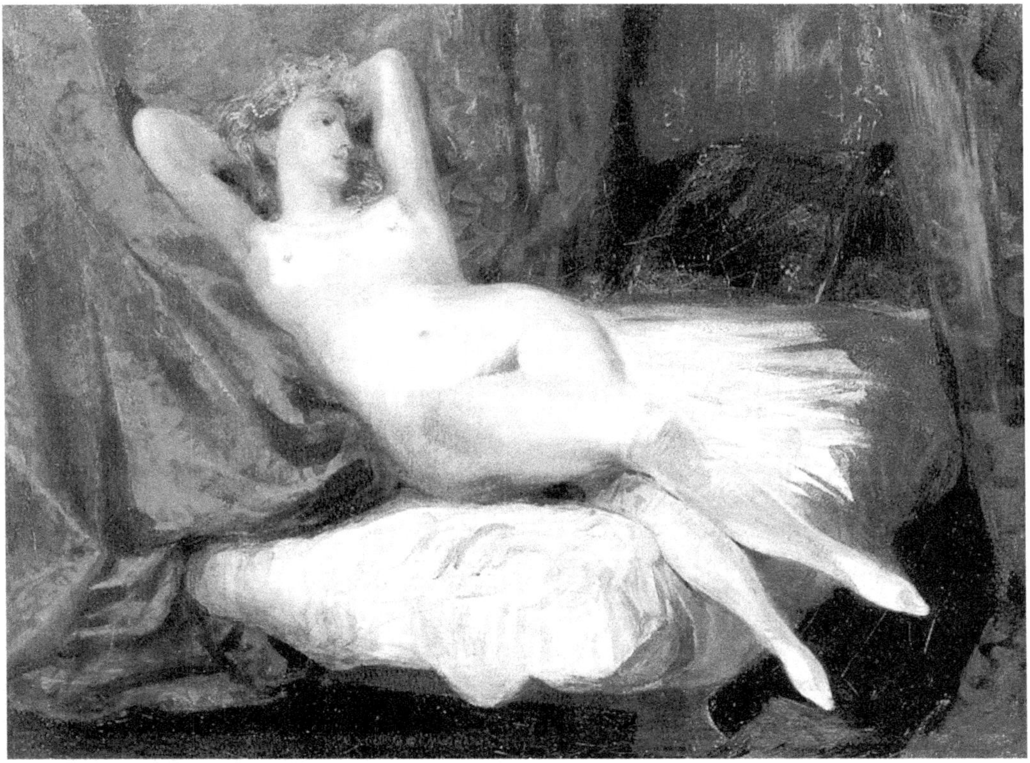

Eugène Delacroix

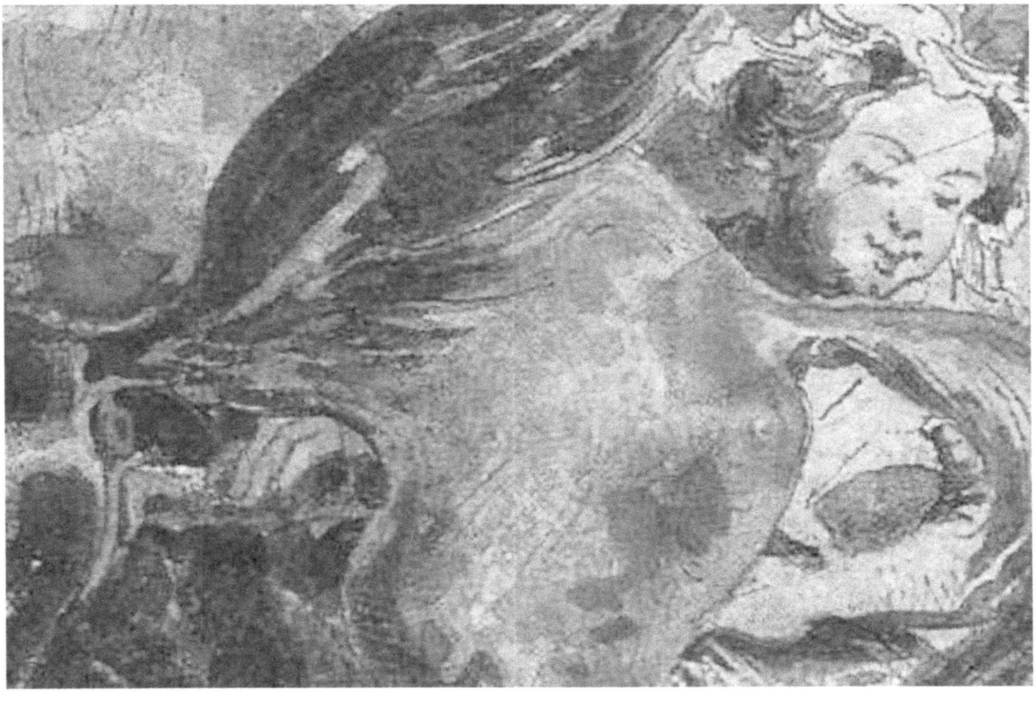

# V

The decoration of the Salon du Roi, which occupied Delacroix from 1833 to 1838, and for which he received the niggardly pay of £1200, was the first great task of this kind entrusted to him. Nevertheless he knew how to adapt design and colour to the architectural conditions in a manner that could scarcely have been bettered by life-long experience. And these conditions were by no means favourable for pictorial decoration, since the walls of the square room are pierced all round by real and blind windows and doors, and the lighting is about as bad as could be. Delacroix's scheme consists of eight large single figures in grisaille for the pilasters; a continuous band, with figure compositions, connecting the spandrils and forming a kind of frieze which is painted in delicate, tender tones, suggestive of faded tapestry, that lead up to the rich colouring of the eight panels in the ceiling and the surround of the skylight. Unfortunately the ceiling is not domed, so that the strong light filtering through the round glazing does not reach the panels and only serves to dazzle one's eyes. It is only by shutting out this central light and by the use of mirrors that it is possible to appreciate the noble, reposeful allegorical groups of *Justice*, *Agriculture*, *Industry*, and *War*, which fill the four oblong panels, and the four graceful Cupids carrying the corresponding attributes in the corners. The frieze, which is divided from the moulding of the ceiling by an ornamental band with appropriate Latin inscriptions, is remarkable for the masterly skill with which the design of the figures and groups is adapted to the awkward shape of the spandrils between the semi-circular arches, and for the lucid clearness of the allegorical representations, the subjects on each wall being closely connected with those on the corresponding panels of the ceiling. Thus under the "Justice" panel are to be seen Truth and Wisdom inspiring a greybeard composing the laws, Meditation interpreting the law, Strength with a tamed lion at the foot of three judges, and the Avenging Angel pursuing two culprits. "Agriculture" is illustrated by a Bacchanalian Vintage Festival, a Harvest scene, and Arcadian figures. "Industry" by allegorical scenes of Commerce, Navigation, and Silk-growing; and "War" by the Manufacture of Arms, and a group of fettered women being taken into captivity. The heroic figures in grisaille on the pilasters are personifications of the Atlantic, the Mediterranean, and the six principal rivers of France, namely the Garonne, the Saone, the Loire, the Rhine (which then belonged to France as much as to Germany), the Seine, and the Rhône.

Before Delacroix had completed the paintings in the Salon du Roi, that is to say in 1837, he was entrusted with the even more important commission for the decoration of the Libraries of the Chamber of Deputies at the Palais Bourbon, and of the Senate at the Luxembourg; three years earlier, in 1834, he had experimented in the technique of fresco painting, which he found more congenial than distemper, when executing three overdoor panels of Leda, Anacreon, and Bacchus, at Valmont, where they still remain *in situ* in all their pristine freshness.

The Library of the Palais Bourbon has been described by a well-known recent German critic as the "French Sistine Chapel." To any one examining this vast work in an unprejudiced spirit it will be difficult to share this enthusiasm. The cool and noble intellectuality which is at the basis of Delacroix's art, even where it is apparently most spontaneous and fugous, certainly renders these decorations supremely interesting. But the appeal is intellectual rather than sensuous. The beholder is filled with profound respect, instead of being thrilled by the emotional effect of colour. Nor can this be entirely due to bad lighting and to the serious deterioration and indifferent restoring of the paintings, of which scarcely more than the design is by Delacroix's own hand, the execution being almost entirely due to Lassalle Bordes and other assistants, who are also largely responsible for the actual painting of the Luxembourg decoration.

The work in the Library of the Chamber of Deputies consists of two hemicycles of "Peace" (Orpheus bringing Civilisation to Greece) and "War" (Attila bringing Barbarism back to Italy), and twenty pendentives – four in each of the five cupolas – with connecting ornamental bands and cartouches. In the first cupola, Poetry is illustrated by "Alexander and Homer's Poems," "The Education of Achilles," "Ovid with the Barbarians," and "Hesiod and the Muse." Theology is the subject of the second dome: "Adam and Eve," "The Babylonian Captivity," "The Death of St. John," and "The Tribute Money." Law of the third: "Numa and Egeria," "Lycurgus," "Demosthenes," and "Cicero"; Philosophy of the fourth: "Herodotus," "Chaldean Shepherd Astronomers," "Seneca's Death," and "Socrates"; and Science of the fifth: "The Death of Pliny," "Aristoteles," "Hippocrates," and "Archimedes." Each pendentive depicts, not a single figure, but an admirably composed scene of history or legend. The series was commenced in 1837 and completed in 1847. The two hemicycles are painted in the encaustic manner direct upon the wall, whilst all the rest is executed in oils on canvas.

The decoration of the Library in the Luxembourg Palace took from 1845 to 1847. It consists of a fan-shaped hemicycle of over 30 feet in width, the subject of which is Alexander, after the Battle of Arbela, ordering the works of Homer to be enclosed in a golden casket captured from the Persians; and the paintings in the cupola – a composition in four parts but without division (Dante presented to Homer by Virgil, a group of Greek philosophers, Orpheus charming the beasts, and illustrious Romans), and four pendentives, St. Jerome, Cicero, Orpheus, and the Muse of Aristoteles.

Earlier in date than the Library of the Senate is the large mural painting in wax colours of the "Pietà" in the Church of St. Dénis-du-Saint-Sacrement. It bears the date 1843, and is, apart from the passionate intensity of movement and expression, and its linear rhythm, interesting as an instance of the almost incredible rapidity with which Delacroix proceeded upon the actual execution of his paintings, once the scheme had taken definite shape in his mind. According to Moreau, who had this information from the artist himself, the whole painting of about 15 ft. by 11 ft. was finished in seventeen days, each day's progress being marked by Delacroix on the wall.

The decoration of the two Libraries was scarcely finished when two new commissions of equal importance gave him further opportunity for the triumphant display of his decorative genius. A few sketches and engravings are unfortunately all that is left to us of the circular centre, the eight shaped oblong panels and the eleven lunettes which constituted the pictorial decoration of the Salon de la Paix at the old Hôtel de Ville, since the building was destroyed by fire in May 1871 in the days of the Commune. Delacroix worked on these designs from 1849 to 1853, and was only paid £1200 for the whole series.

If the labour and thought expended upon the Salon de la Paix were destined to lead to such short-lived results, the magnificent centrepiece of the ceiling in the Salon d'Apollon can be seen to-day in its unimpaired freshness – the most striking testimony to its creator's genius. The decoration of this gallery was entrusted to Le Brun as far back as 1661; and it was Louis XIV.'s favourite painter who conceived the idea of paying homage to his master, the "Roi Soleil," by depicting "The Triumph of Apollo" in the centre panel, with appropriate subjects in the other ten compartments. But his work was interrupted, when he was called upon to supervise the decoration of Versailles, before he had even sketched out the design for "The Triumph of Apollo." The ten minor compartments remained neglected for over a century, and were allowed to get into a deplorable condition, until the restoration was taken in hand in 1848, the painting of the great centre being at the same time entrusted to Delacroix. Apart from the fact that Apollo was to be the hero of the design, Delacroix had an entirely free hand, and chose to depict the god vanquishing the Python, with Diana, Mercury, Minerva, Hercules, Vulcan, Boreas, Zephyrus, Victory, Iris, and Nymphs as subsidiary figures. Although the design offends against the fundamental rule of all ceiling decorations, that there should be no "above" and "below," and that the composition should be devised so as to be equally intelligible from every point of view, one cannot but admire the noble co- and subordination of the different groups and figures, the lucid clearness of the pictorial statement of an essentially intellectual conception, the astonishing colour-magic, and, above all, the manner in which the master has adapted his own work to the somewhat gaudy and over-decorated surroundings. "Delacroix," says Robaut in his "Catalogue Raisonné," "has here shown himself as great in execution as in invention, and the Apollo ceiling is one of the most perfect works of art that reflect glory upon all the centuries" – a judgment which has been endorsed by two generations of artists and critics. The ceiling, for which the master was paid the sum of £960, was finished in 1849. About two hundred sketches and drawings for details of the composition figured in the sale held after Delacroix's death.

We have seen that from the time when Delacroix began his work for the Salon du Roi in 1833 until the completion of the Salon de la Paix in 1853, he had no sooner brought any of his monumental decorations to a successful conclusion when some other decorative work was entrusted to him. And so again, in 1853, when he had just finished the Hôtel de Ville series, he was made to proceed immediately upon that great fresco decoration of the Chapel of the Saints-Anges at St. Sulpice, which, completed in 1861, was his last work of real importance, and is in many respects the crowning achievement of his great career. Here, for once, Delacroix found himself able to work under conditions similar to those under which the Florentine masters of the quattrocento wrought their marvellous frescoes. Here was no complete scheme of ornate architectural details, no sumptuous framework in which spaces had been left for the addition of painted panels that had to be treated in a more or less florid manner to fit into their rich surroundings. Here everything was left to the painter's free will, checked only by the consideration of the fitness of the subjects for the site and by the architectural proportions of the little chapel. And it is not too much to say that Delacroix solved the problem in more masterly fashion than any painter between the glorious days of the Italian Renaissance and the advent of Puvis de Chavannes, the greatest decorator of modern times.

Like all true fresco decoration, the two large paintings of "Jacob wrestling with the Angel" and "Heliodorus driven from the Temple" do not attempt to give the illusion of plastic life, or of an opening cut through the wall, but duly accentuate the flatness of the surface. The scale of colour adopted for this admirable decoration aims, without the least sense of monotony or dulness, at the exquisiteness of the greens and greys of a fine panel of faded Flemish tapestry, and has nothing in common with the rich, glowing palette which Delacroix had inherited from Rubens and the Venetian colourists. The tapestry-like effect is particularly noticeable in the treatment of the trees which are so important a feature in the composition of "Jacob wrestling with the Angel," the figures being comparatively small in scale, though by no means subordinate to the landscape. Nothing could be more impressive than the contrast of the terrific muscular exertion of Jacob and the easy grace with which it is made ineffective by his invincible supernatural opponent. The group is one of the noblest creations of modern art – worthy of the brush of a Pollaiuolo or a Signorelli.

In the "Heliodorus" the accidents of Nature's architecture are replaced by the equally imposing but deliberate and formal lines of the architecture created by human builders. The general disposition of the design is not unlike that of the earlier "Justice of Trajan"; but there is this significant difference between the earlier work and the St. Sulpice fresco, that the very first glance reveals the essentially human element in the first, and the irresistible force of the supernatural in the second. The tempestuous, sweeping onrush of the two flying angels contrasted with the calm consciousness of all-conquering strength expressed not only in the mounted heavenly messenger but in the very action of his noble horse – the horses in Delacroix's paintings invariably reflect the mood of the drama or tragedy that forms the subject of the picture – are a pictorial conception of unsurpassed grandeur. The only unsatisfactory part of the St. Sulpice decoration is the ceiling, where St. Michael is depicted overthrowing the Demon. Probably the execution of this oval composition was almost entirely the work of assistants, as Delacroix's failing health, aggravated by lead poisoning caused by the extensive use of white of lead paint in his large decorations, would not have allowed him to work under such fatiguing conditions as are unavoidable in painting a ceiling *in situ*.

The frescoes in the Chapel of the Saints-Anges were the swan-song of Delacroix's genius. In the two years that followed their completion, he still continued to paint and to draw – the practice of his art was for him the very breath of life – but he produced nothing that need be considered in the record of his achievement. In March 1863, the affection of his eyes, of which he had suffered intermittently for years, took a turn for the worse. On the 26th of May he left Paris for Champrosay, but during the journey had a severe attack of hemorrhage of the lungs, which recurred five days later; and he had to be taken back to Paris. His illness became worse and worse, and after a month he was taken back to the country, only to be sent back again to Paris on July 14. His days were counted. He took to his bed immediately upon his arrival, and breathed his last at six o'clock in the morning on August 13, 1863.

# VI

How strangely Delacroix's art was misunderstood by his contemporaries who, nurtured on the tinted cartoons of the ruling School, stood aghast before the passionate utterance of the master's "intoxicated broom," or, assuming the role of Beckmesser, marked with offensive rap of chalk on the blackboard of the public Press his sins against their dogmatic rules. In their blindness they even went so far as to accuse him of being unable to draw! What seemed altogether to escape their perception, was that the fiery impulse, the tempestuous *élan* of Delacroix's romantic imagination was largely controlled by his cool intellectuality. Delacroix was a thinker and a man of profound culture. He had, moreover, the greatest respect for tradition. If, in the actual painting of his pictures, he was carried away by his enthusiasm and worked like one inspired, he never started upon this the final stage without an enormous amount of preparatory sketches for every figure, every detail – never before the idea had taken firm and definite shape in his mind. The sweep of the brush, the vitalising amplifications and elements of movement may have been left to the inspiration of the moment; but chance played no part in the disposition of the design and the arrangement of the colour-scheme.

It was that amplification and exaggeration of forms, by which alone movement can be expressed in art, that led the unthinking to the belief that Delacroix "could not draw." Of course, the application of Ingres's standard of classic perfection in drawing might justify the conclusion, but one need only glance at Delacroix's sketch-books and studies to realise that he was a great draughtsman, if drawing, as it was to him, is considered the means towards an end, and not an end in itself. And his mastery of spontaneous, nervously expressive drawing was as complete as it could be, if mastery can be acquired through the curbing of impetuous genius by half a century's methodical, steady practice. For Delacroix, from his early student days to his death, never started on his day's work without having first "got his hand in" by half-an-hour's practice in sketching or drawing, just as a pianist will first run through his finger exercises and scales, to make sure of his mastery over his instrument.

Thus, by unremitting practice, Delacroix acquired such absolute command of the language of line and form that, in the pictorial expression of his ideas, he used it as an orator uses the language of words – in a steady flow, without doubts and hesitations. His inspiration was not checked and weakened by the struggle for an adequate form of expression. There was nothing in life and in nature that did not stimulate his artistic curiosity, and all his sketches betray the same passionate search for the really essential, the elements of life and movement and mood, which are often to be obtained only by the sacrifice of literal correctness. He never tired of making drawings after Rembrandt's etchings, and he spent many hours at the Jardin des Plantes, in the company of the animal sculptor Barye, sketching and painting wild beasts from life. Indeed, Delacroix was rarely rivalled, and probably never surpassed, as a painter of animals either in repose or in the very frenzy of movement.

His astonishing rapidity of production has already been exemplified by his painting of the large "Pietà" at St. Dénis-du-Saint-Sacrement in seventeen days. An even more striking instance is afforded by the "King Rodrigo losing his Crown," now in the Cheramy Collection. A number of artists had agreed to contribute towards the decoration of a room in a villa taken by

Alexandre Dumas père in 1830. Delacroix was of their number; and the day agreed for the completion of the pictures was to be celebrated by a ball. When Delacroix arrived at midday of the day in question he found that all the panels were in their proper places, leaving only an unexpectedly large gap for his own contribution. "He had meant only to paint a few flowers. 'Listen,' said Dumas, 'I have just been reading something that will do for you,' and he described the first canto of the 'Romancero,' in which Rodrigo loses his crown. Delacroix began at once, and had painted the whole scene by sunset, in the most unusual colours, a harmony in yellow, unique in his work. Great was the enthusiasm in the evening when the friends saw the picture; Barye, in particular, who had contributed an excellent panel, is said to have been beside himself."[1]

Delacroix's life, apart from his struggle for recognition – a struggle which he fought entirely with his brush, leaving the controversial side to others – was singularly uneventful. His only passions were his art, his love of romantic literature, and his staunch friendship. A few journeys and frequent spells of illness were the only events that broke the even tenor of his life. As a writer, Delacroix has left a marvellous "Journal," which ought to be consulted and carefully studied by every artist, and a number of carefully constructed magazine articles on various æsthetic questions, which only reveal the cool intellectual side of his dual nature. He was a man of great reticence, who rarely allowed himself to be drawn into criticising the art of his contemporaries. In his critical comments on the masters – even on those whose style was diametrically opposed to his own temperament – he always proved himself keenly appreciative of their great qualities. Strangely enough, Delacroix, who is considered the leader, and certainly was one of the main inspirers of the Romanticist movement, not only disliked the application of this term to his own art, but had little sympathy with the Romanticist literature of his own time and country. His attitude towards Victor

1 Julius Meier-Graefe, "Modern Art," vol. i.

Hugo almost amounted to hostility; and he always treated Baudelaire, who had espoused his cause with keen enthusiasm, with the most calculated reserve. In music his tastes were severely classical – "he refreshed himself with Mozart, was never quite able to convert himself to Beethoven, abhorred the modern French composers, and was the first to condemn Wagner."

If Delacroix, except for a very brief period at the beginning of his career, never suffered real poverty, he, on the other hand, never received adequate pecuniary reward for his work. To the very end he was forced to sell his finest pictures at ridiculously inadequate prices; and on some of his large decorative commissions he found himself actually out of pocket. It was probably the conviction that posthumous justice would inevitably be done to his genius, which made him insist in his will upon the sale of his remaining works by public auction. And events proved that he was right. The sale, which was held from February 16-29, 1864, was estimated to produce about £4000, but resulted in a total of close upon £13,500.

The instructions about his burial, left by Delacroix in his will, reflect something of his noble aloofness and his respect for great tradition in art. "My tomb shall be in the cemetery of Père-Lachaise, on the height and in a place a little apart. There shall be placed upon it neither emblem, nor bust, nor statue. My tomb shall be copied very exactly from the antique, or Vignole, or Palladio, with very pronounced projections, contrary to all that is done in the architecture of to-day."

Illustrations on the following pages are from some contemporaries
of Eugéne Delacroix.

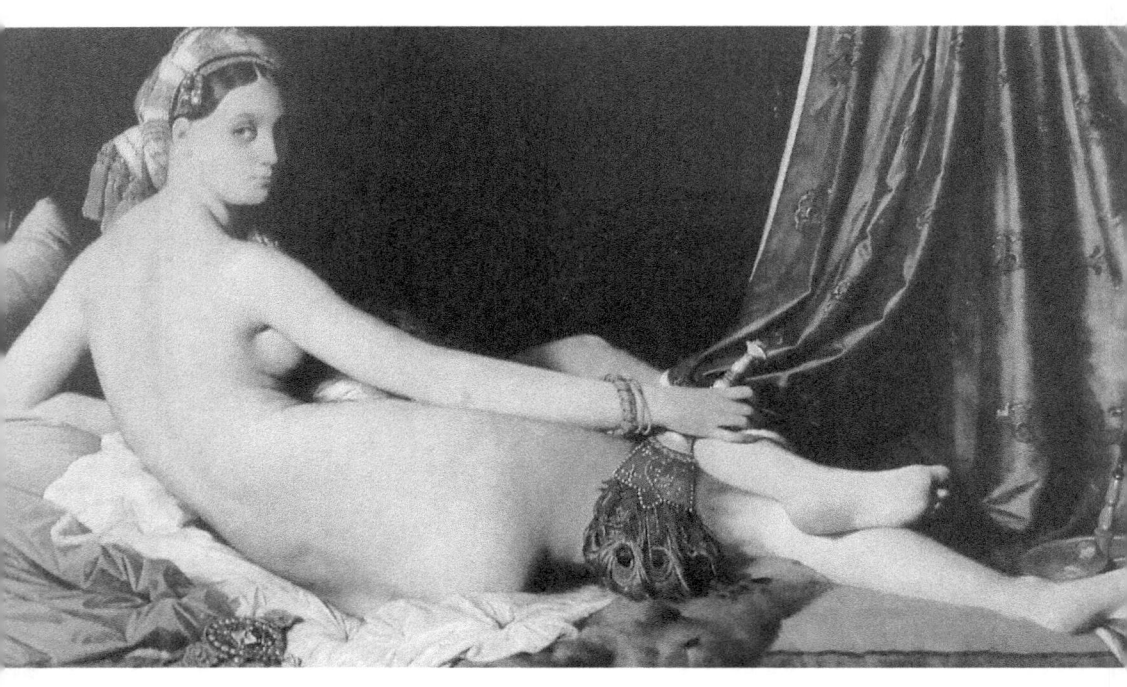

Jean-Dominique Ingres, Grand Odalisque, 1814

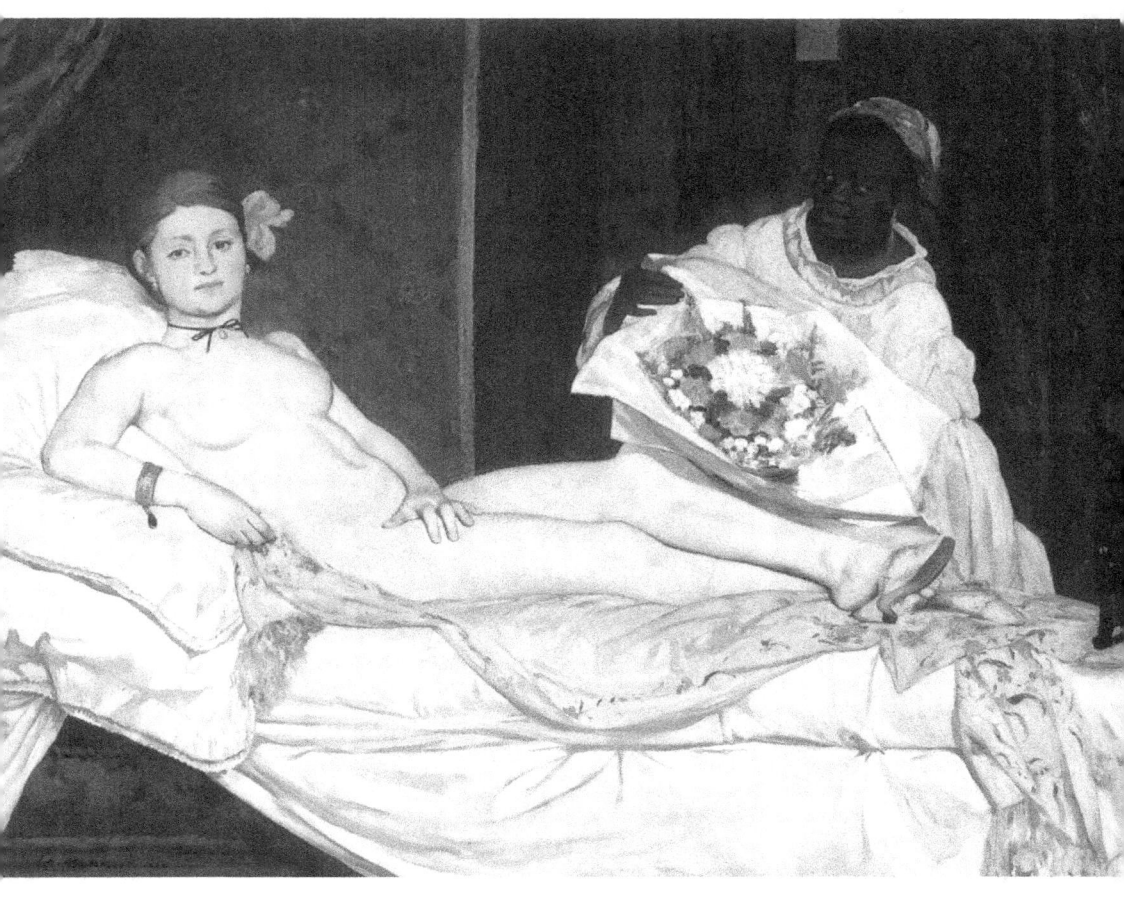

Edouard Manet, Olympia, Musée d'Orsay, Paris

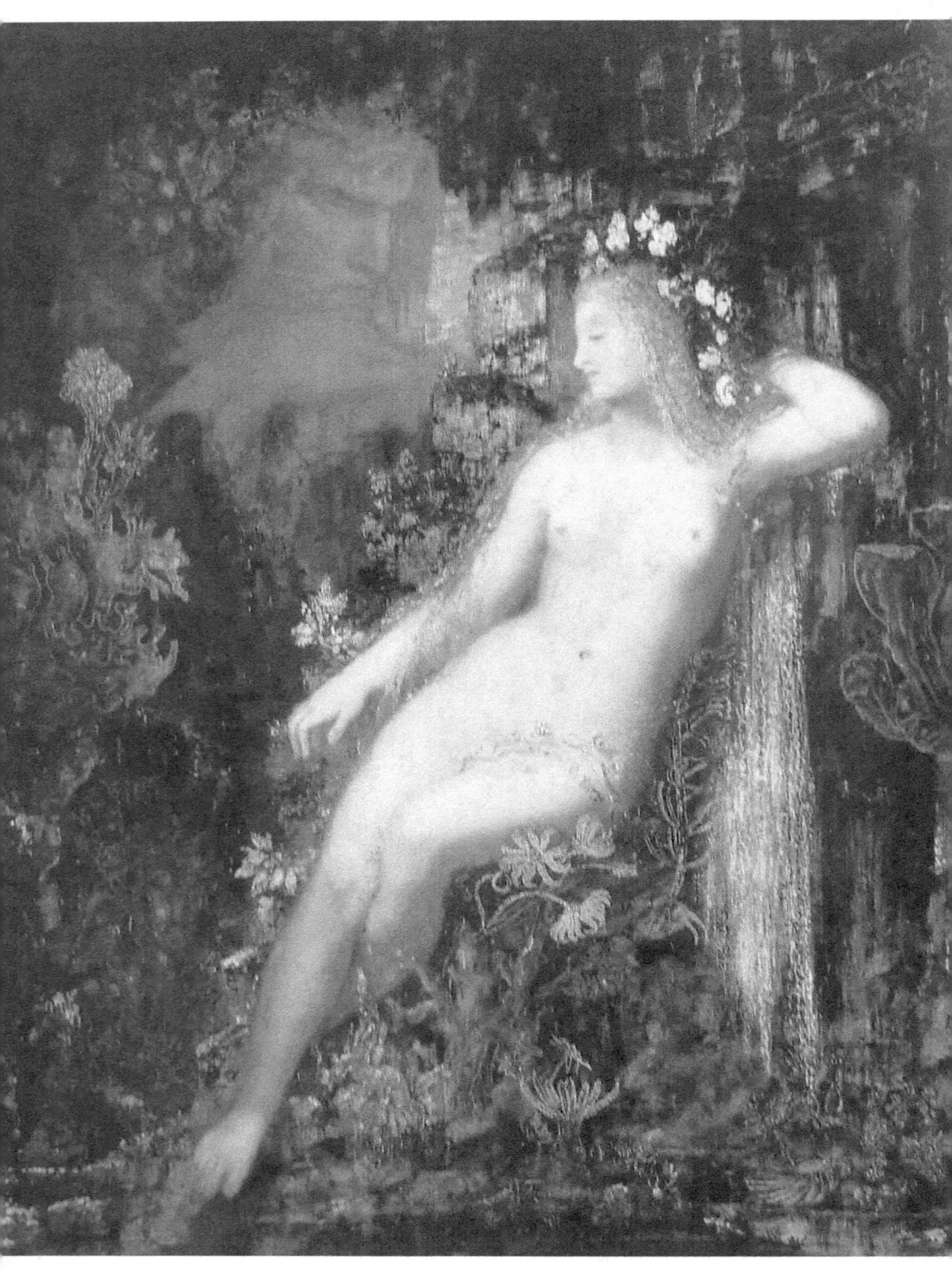

Gustave Moreau, Galatea, 1880

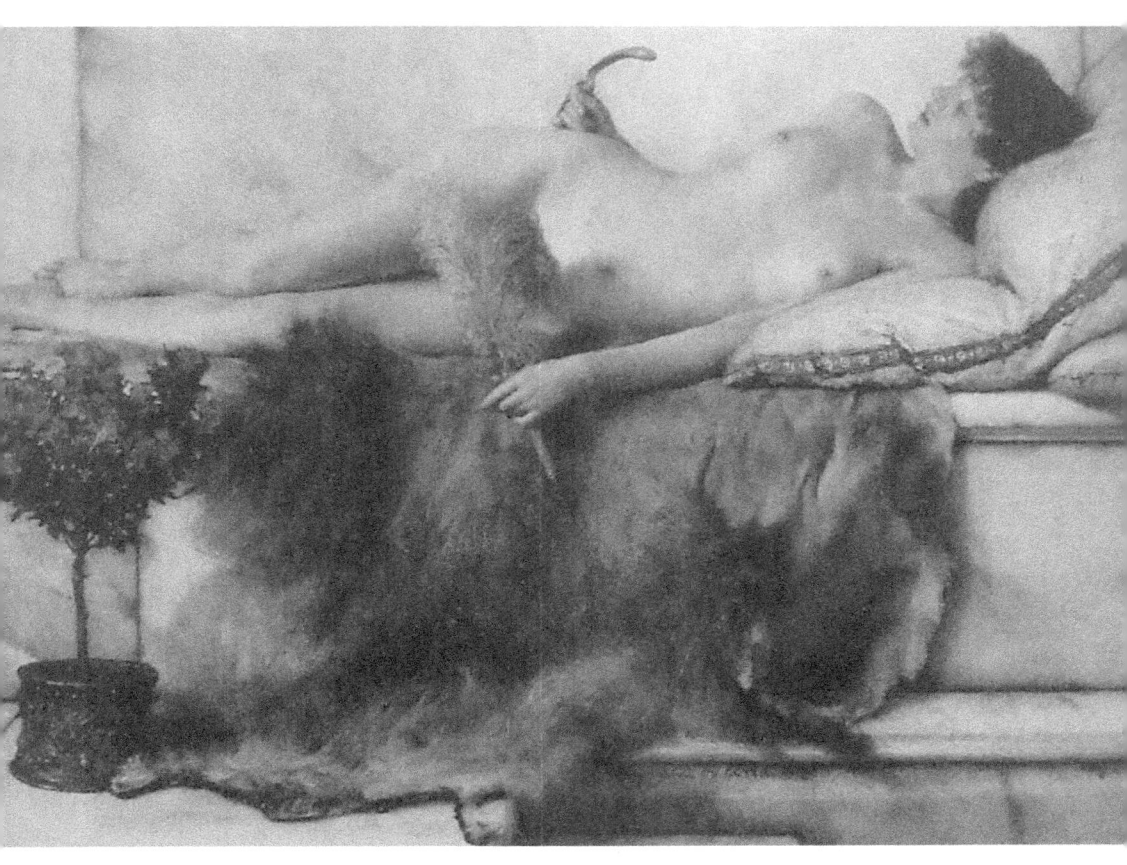

Lawrence Alma-Tadema, In the Tepidarium, 1881,
Lady Lever Art Gallery, Liverpool

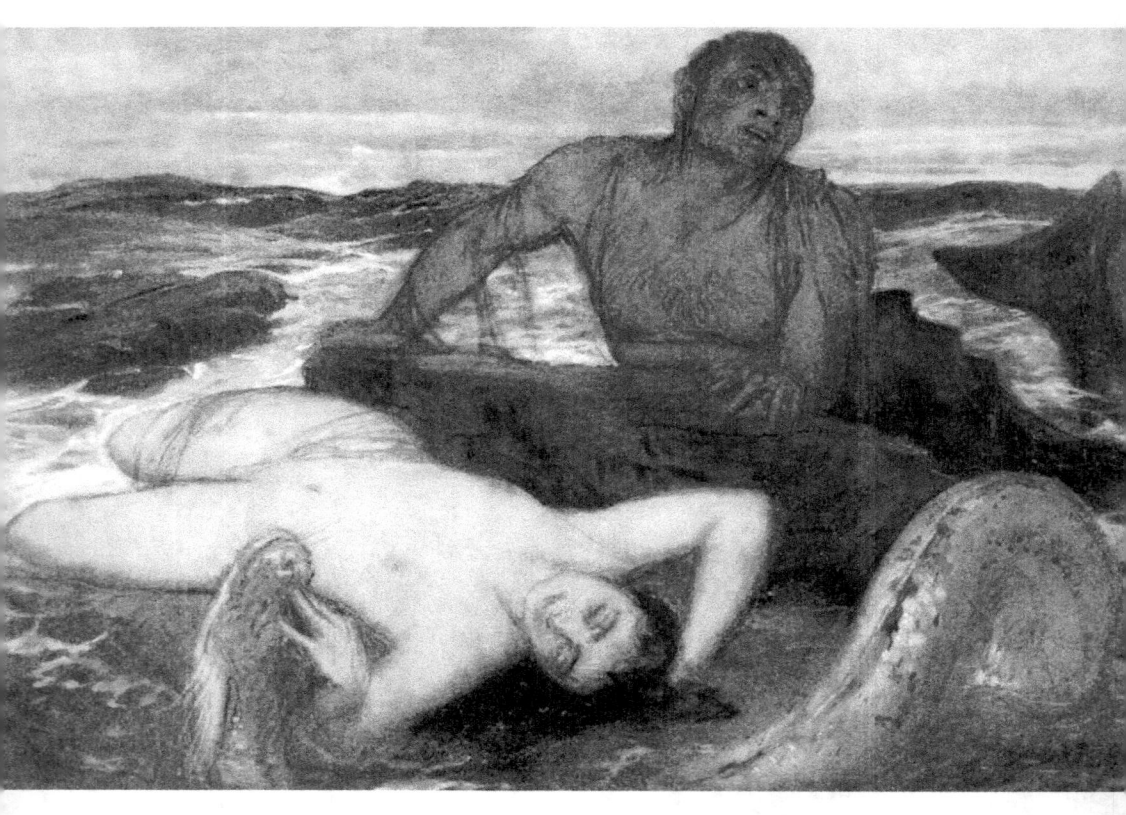

Arnold Böcklin, Triton and Nereid, 1877

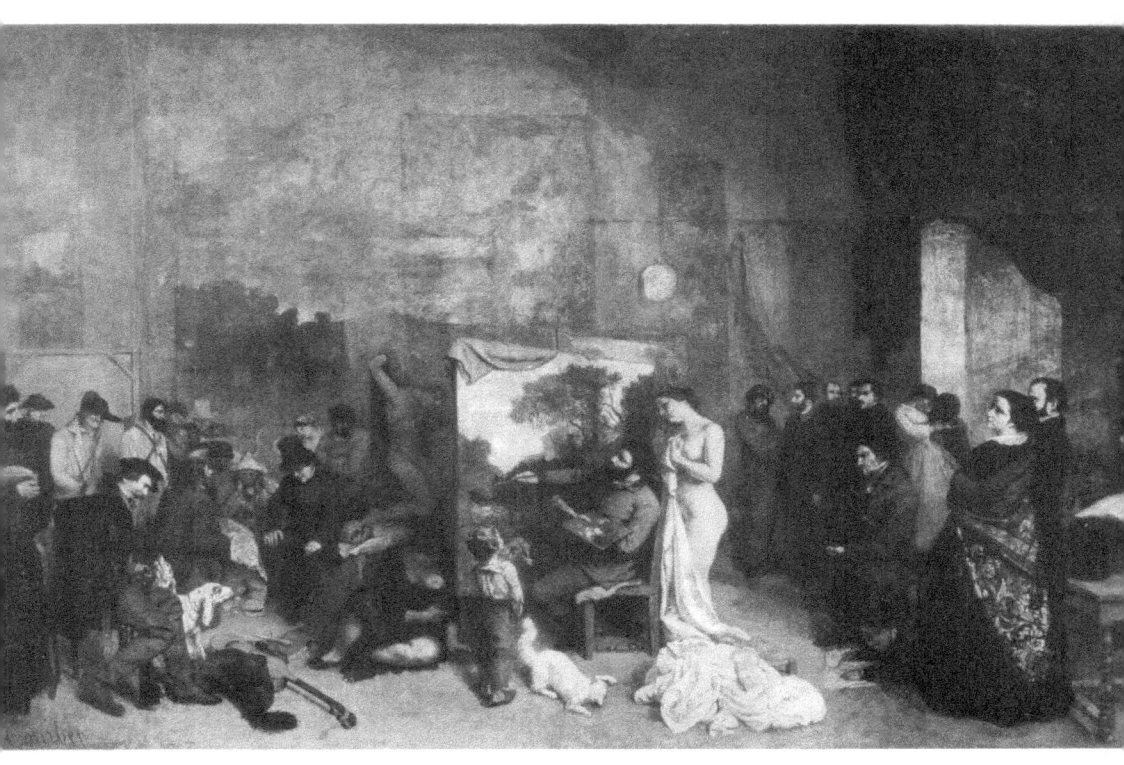

Gustave Courbet, The Studio, 1855, Musée d'Orsay, Paris

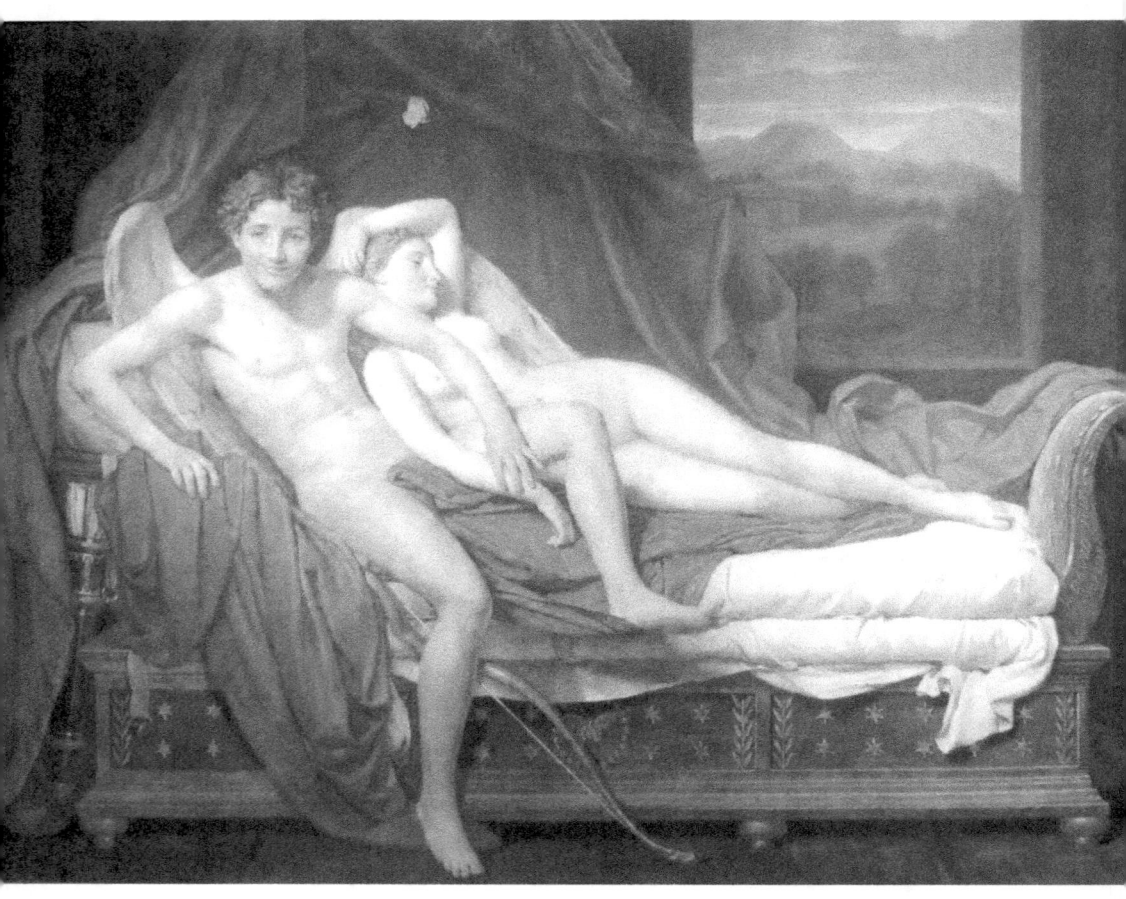

Jacques-Louis David, Cupid and Psyche, 1817,
Cleveland Museum of Art

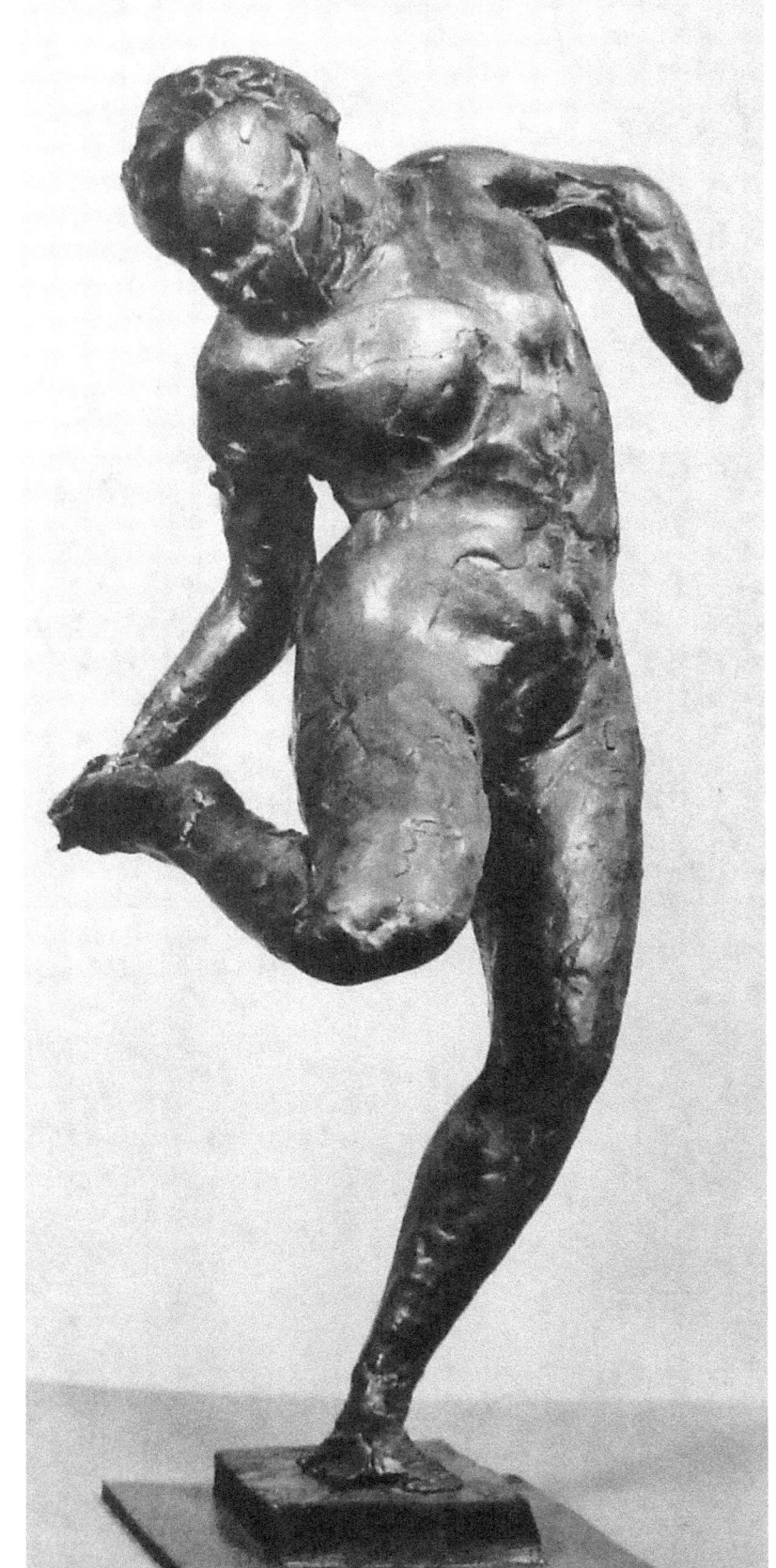

Edgar Degas,
Dancer Looking At
the Sole of Her
Right Foot, 1882-95,
New York

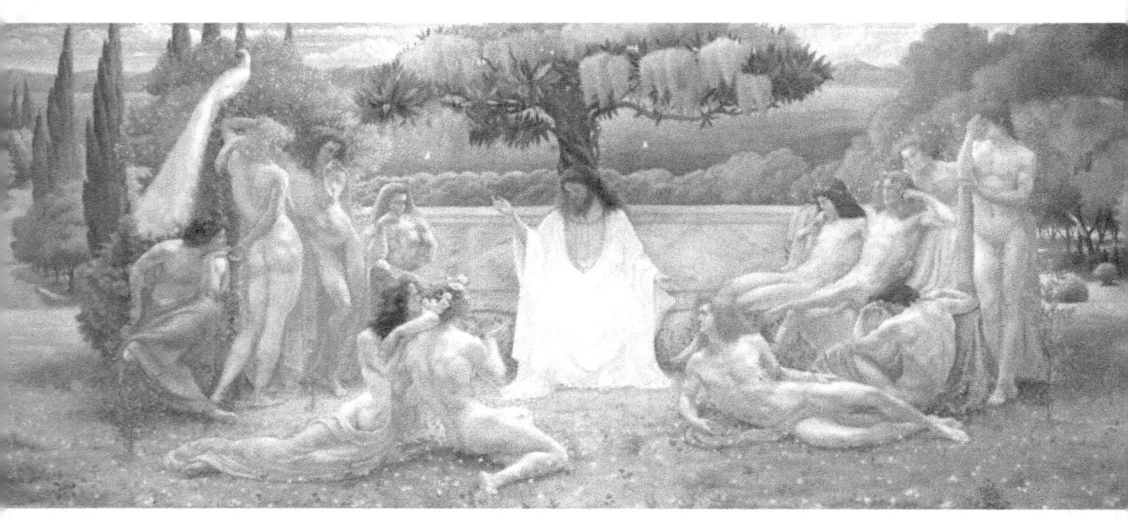

Jean Delville, The School of Plato, 1898

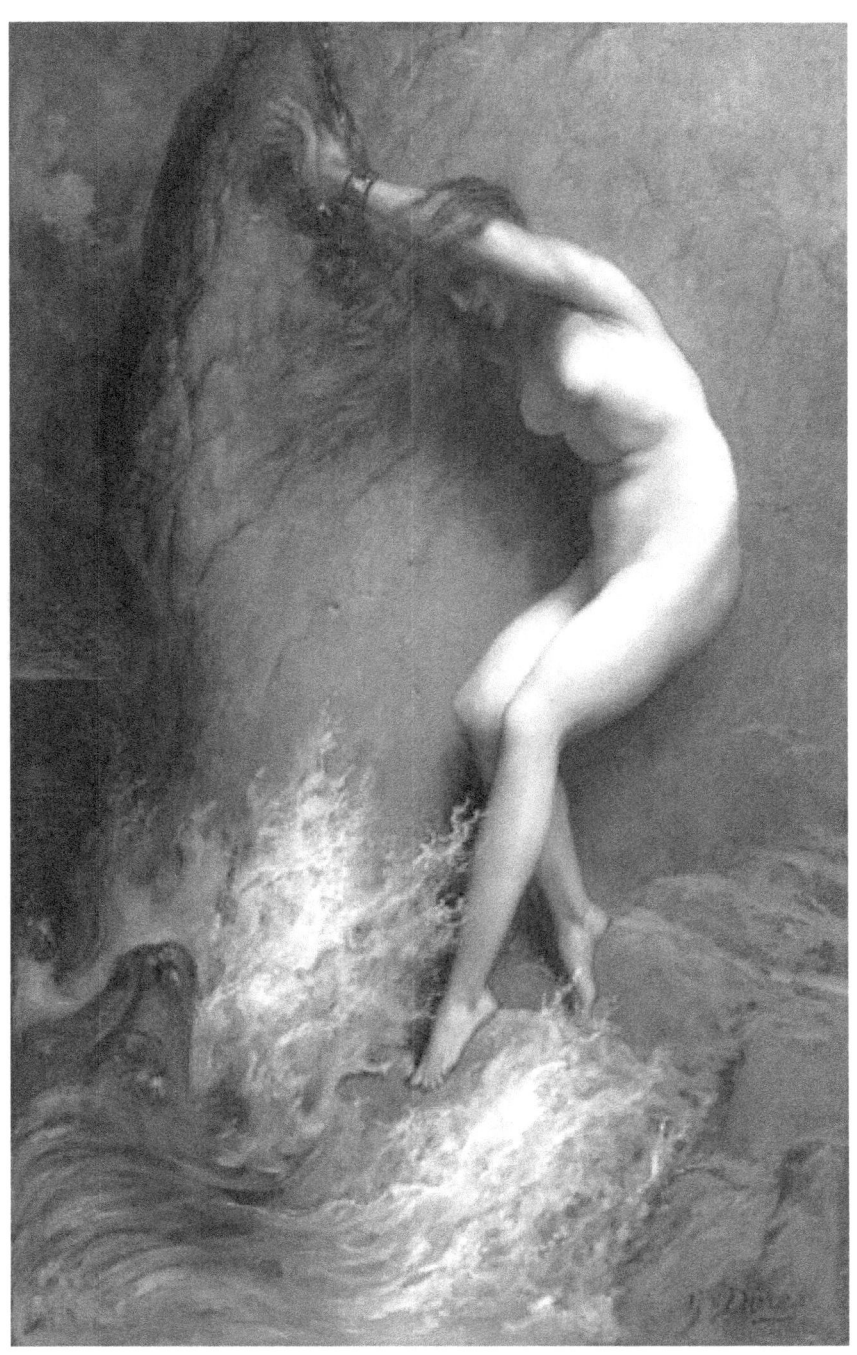

Gustave Doré

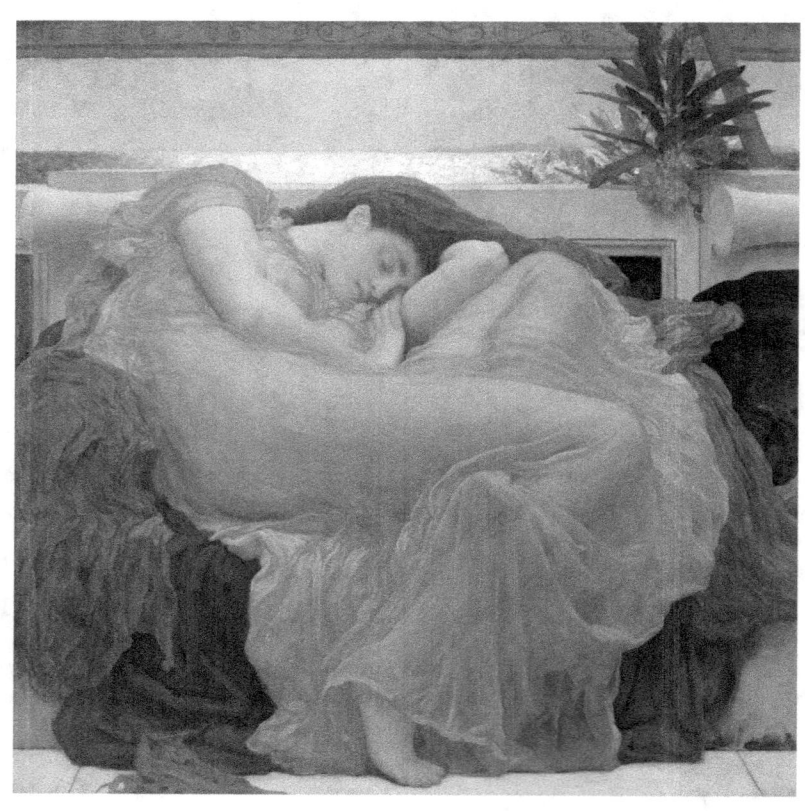

Lord Leighton, Flaming June, 1895, Puerto Rico

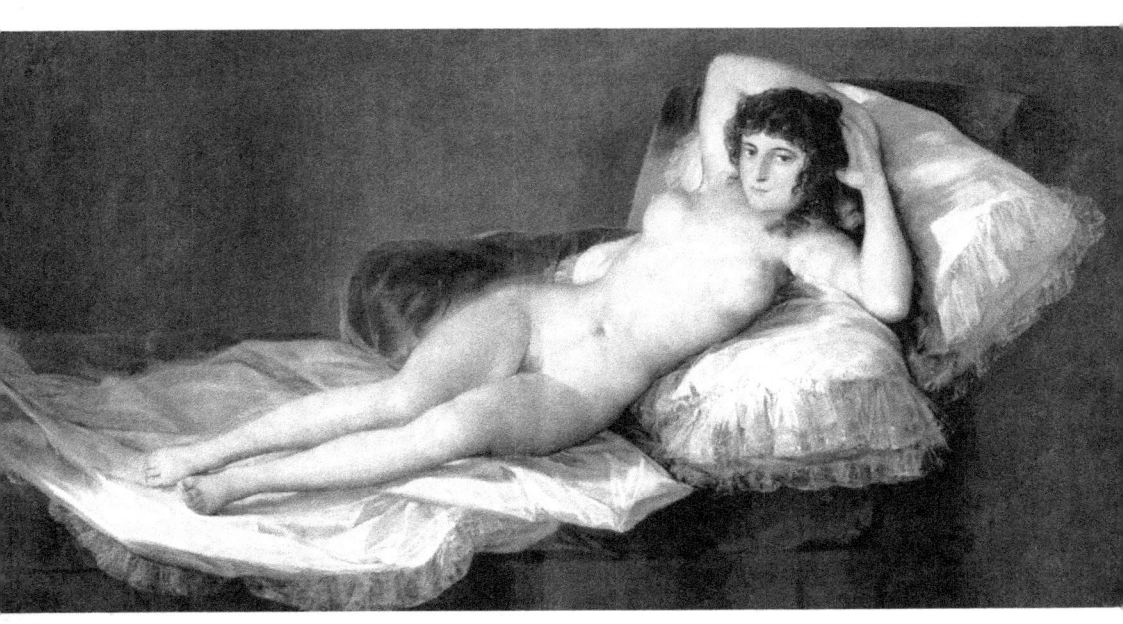

Francisco de Goya, Naked Maja, c. 1801, Prado, Madrid

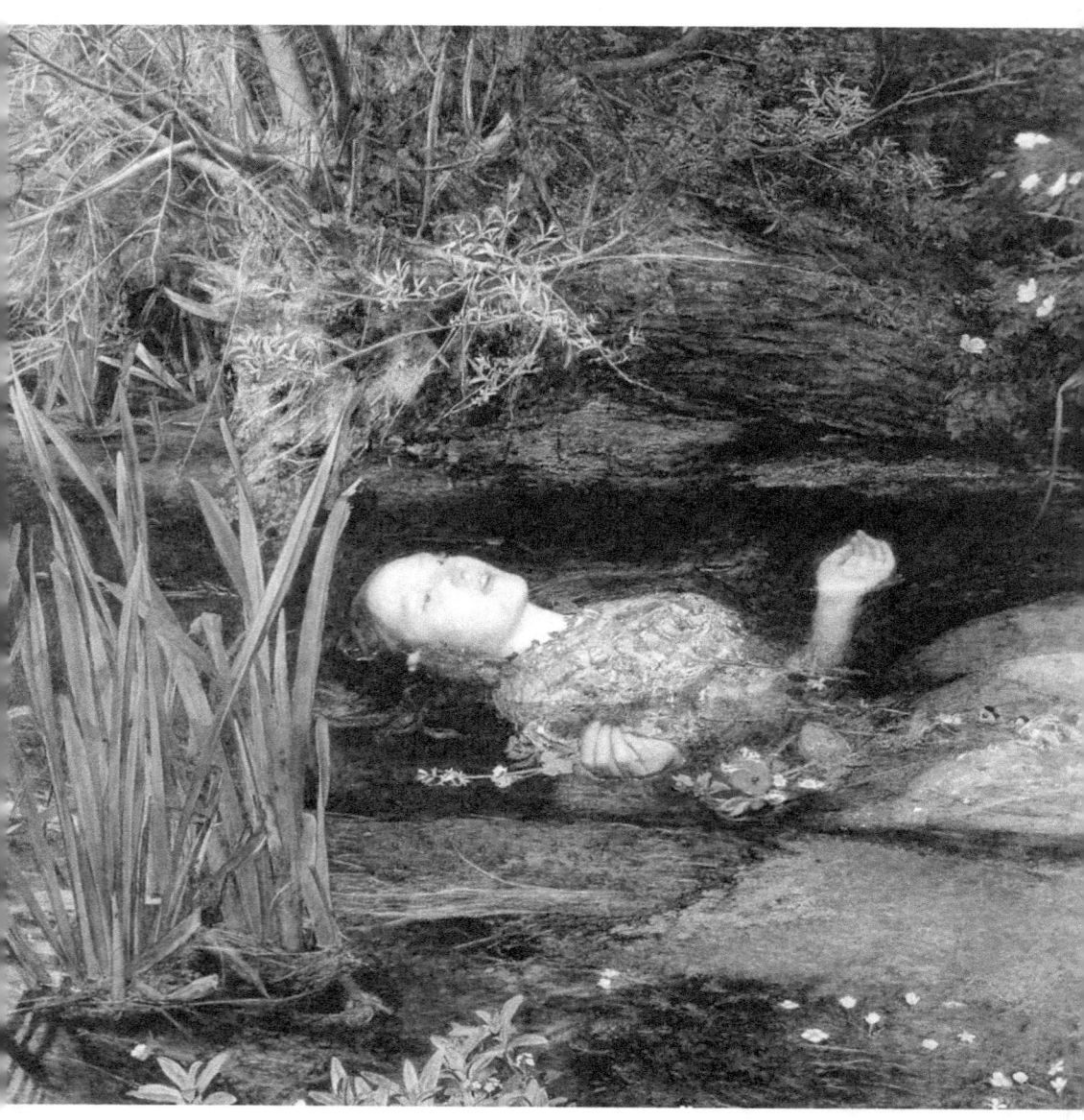

John Everett Millais, Ophelia.

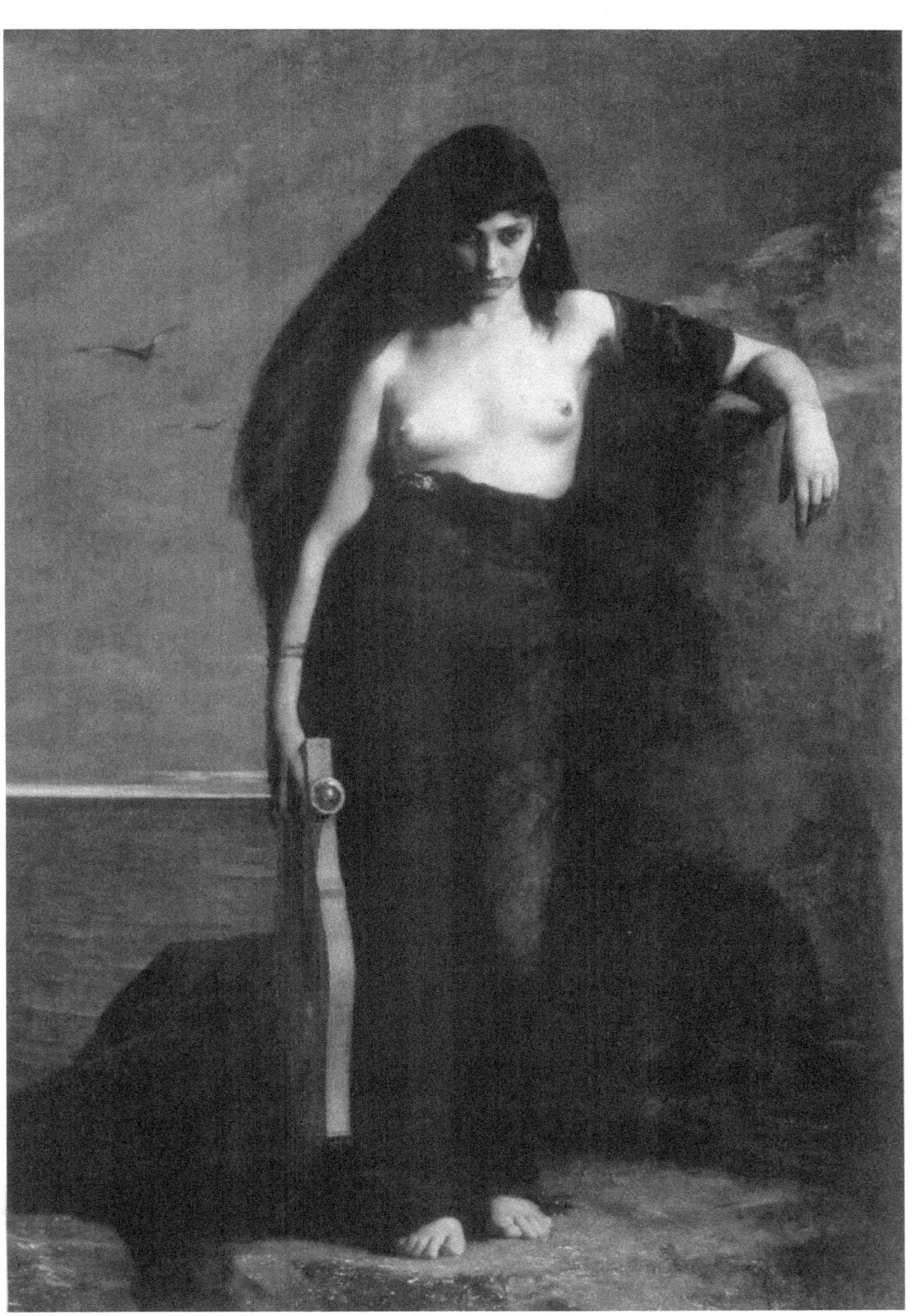

Charles Mengin, Sappho, 1867, Manchester

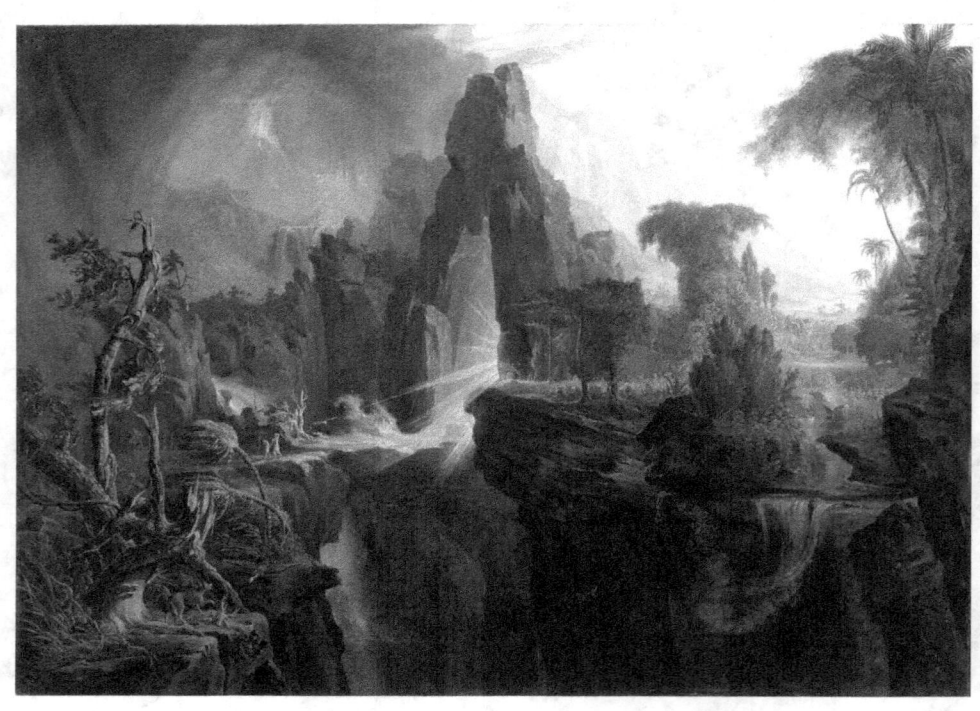

Thomas Cole, Expulsion From the Garden of Eden, 1828,
Museum of Fine Arts, Boston

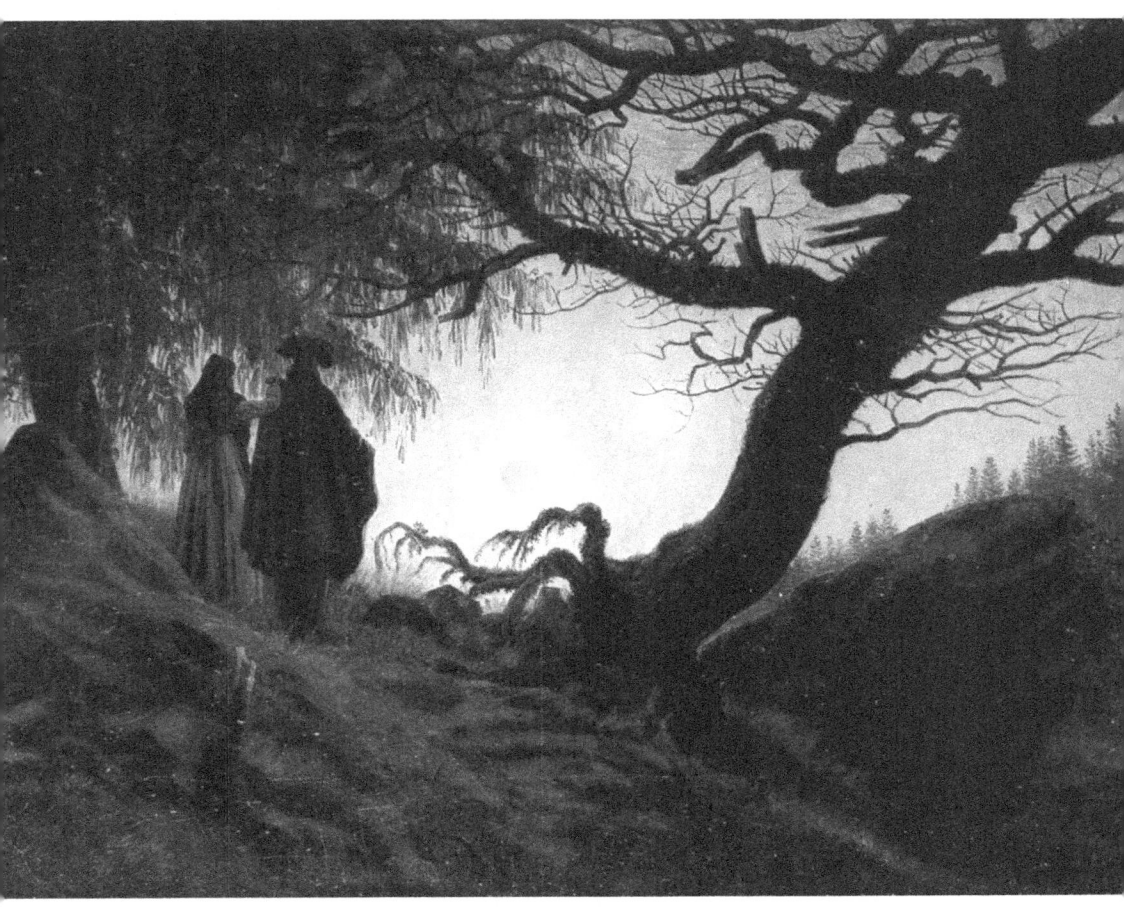

Caspar David Friedrich, Man and
Woman Contemplating the Moon,
1830-35, Alte Nationalgalerie

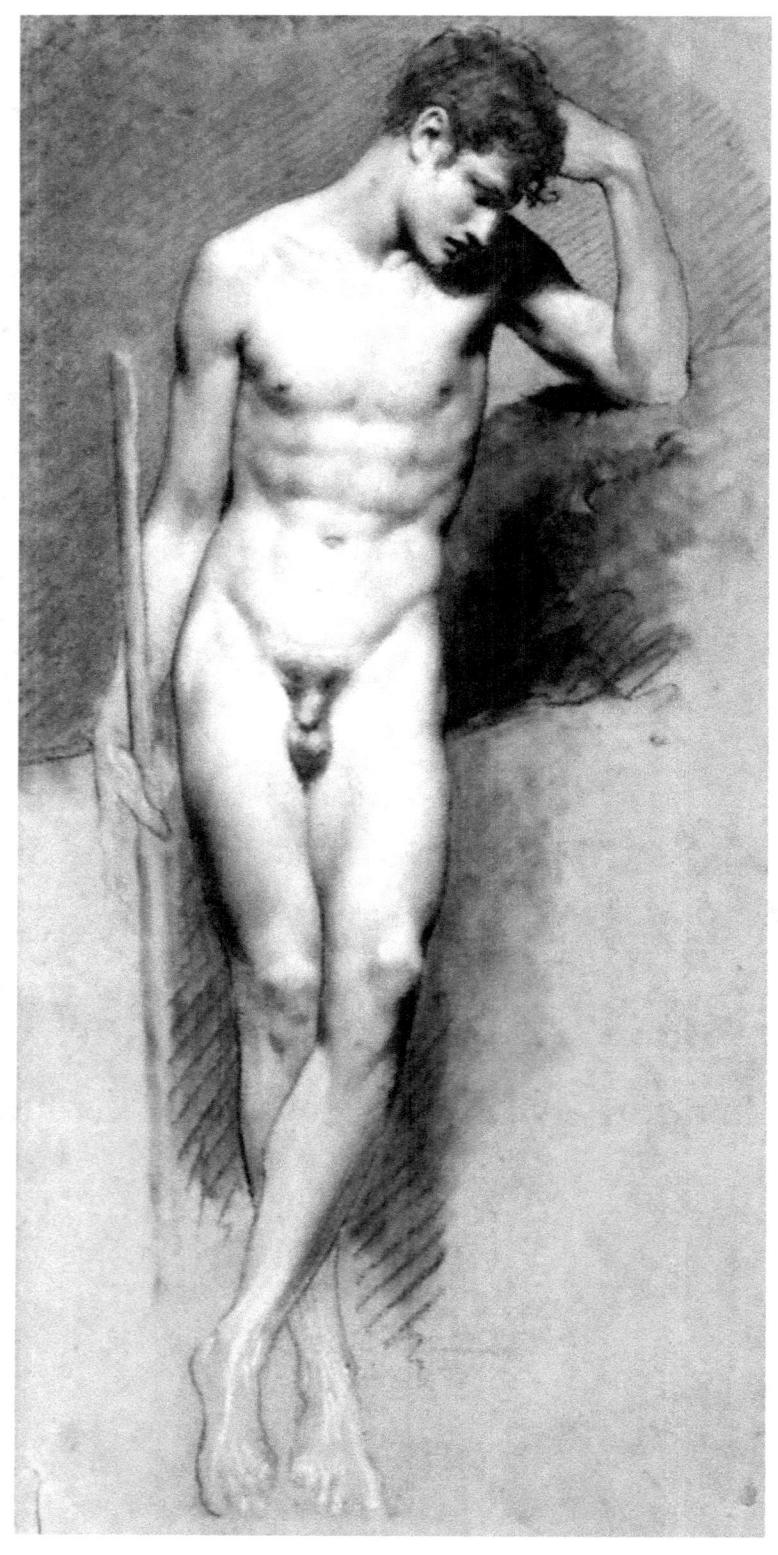

Pierre-Paul Prud'hon (1758-1823), Male Nude Standing

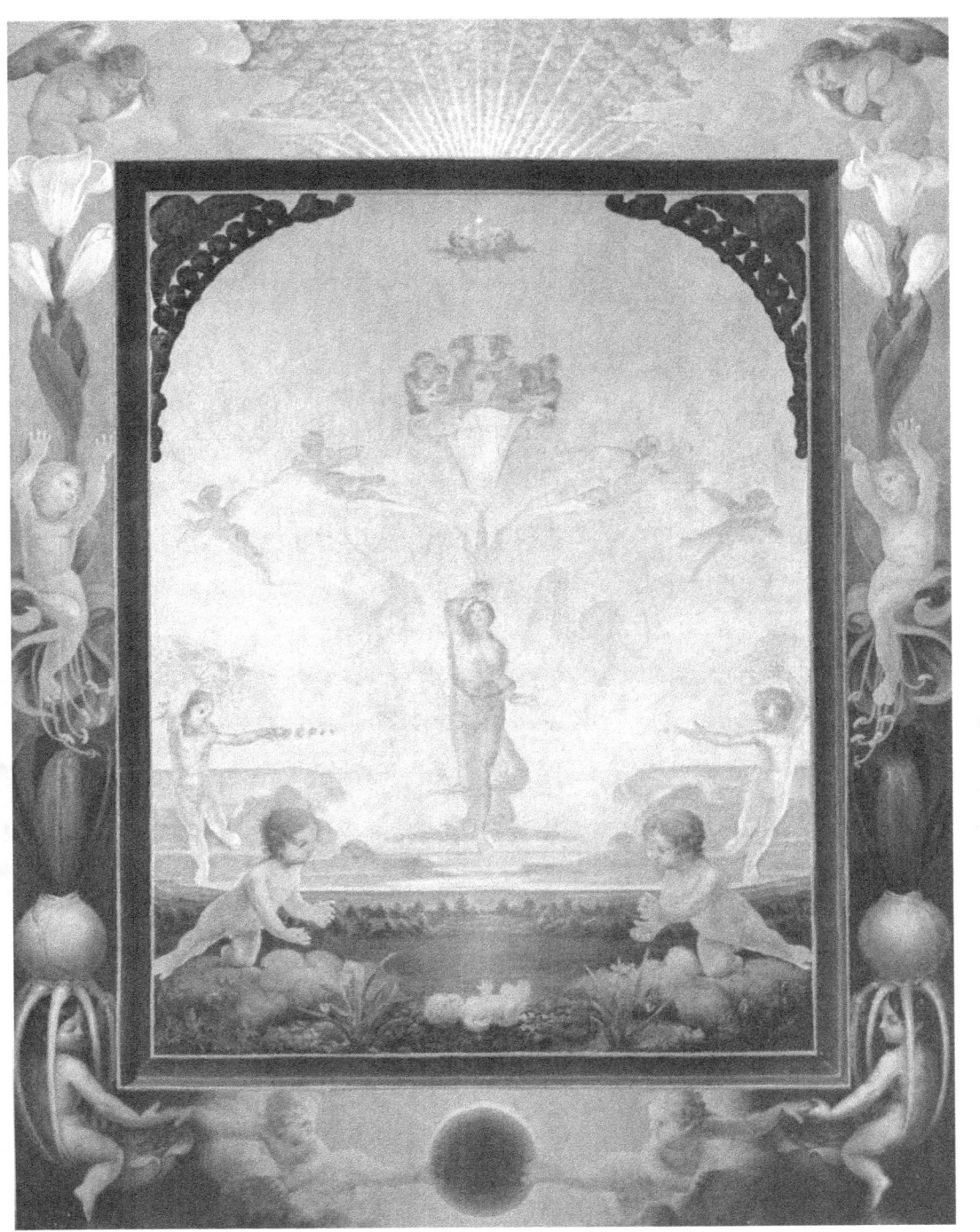

Philipp Otto Runge, Morning, 1808, Hamburg

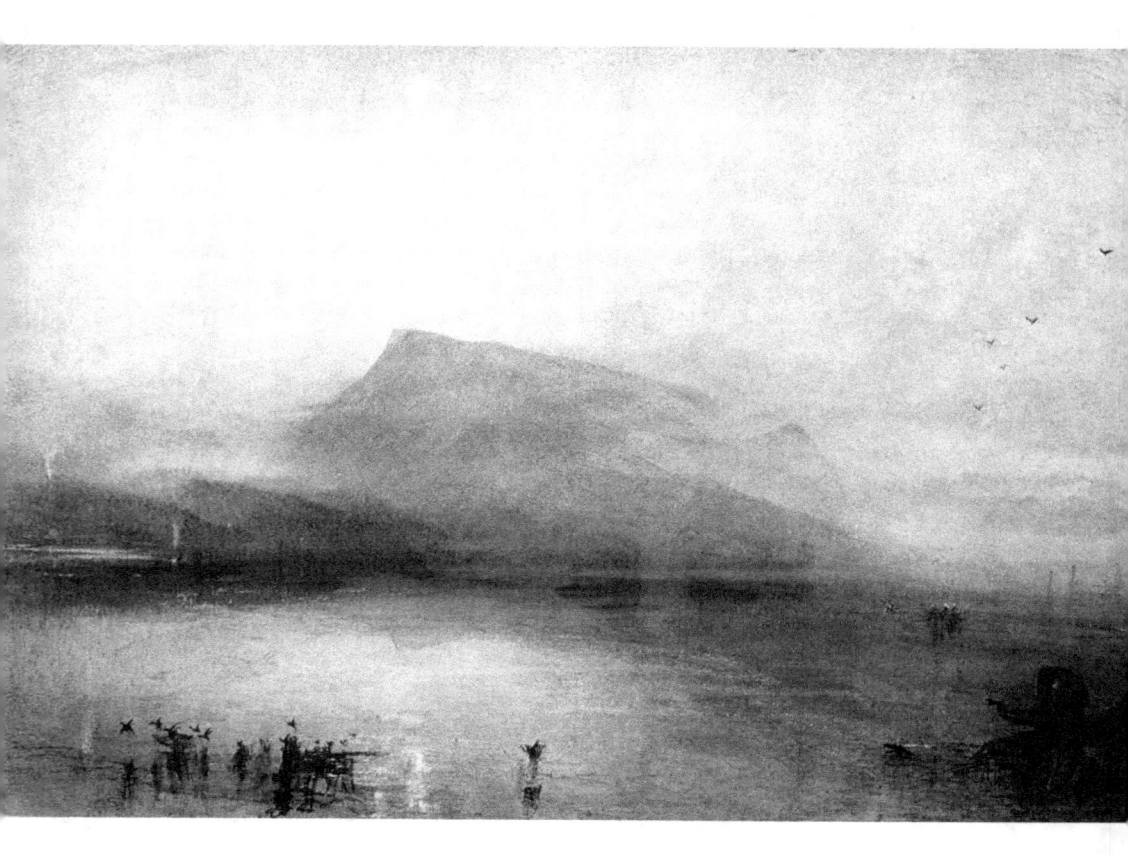

J.M.W. Turner, The Blue Rigi, Lake of Lucerne, Sunrise,
1842, Clore Gallery, London

# NOTES ON WORKS

THE ENTRY OF THE CRUSADERS INTO CONSTANTINOPLE.
(In the Louvre)

Painted in 1841 for the Gallery at Versailles, whence it was subsequently removed to the Louvre, this large, dramatic composition belongs to the period when Delacroix's palette, inspired from the first by Rubens and Veronese, had assumed increased richness under the influence of Eastern light and colour. It is significant of the lack of appreciation shown to the master by his contemporaries, and even by his supporters, that the commission was accompanied by the request that the picture should not look like a Delacroix.

ALGERIAN WOMEN IN THEIR APARTMENT
(In the Louvre)

This picture was one of the first-fruits of Delacroix's journey to Morocco with Count Mornay's mission. It was painted in 1833, the year after his return to France, commissioned by the State at the price of 3000 frs. The handling of the upright figure of the negress suggests Spanish influence, and was in turn obviously well known to Manet when he painted his "Olympia."

THE DEATH OF OPHELIA
(In the Louvre)

This is one, and perhaps the most successful of many slightly varying versions of the same subject, which the artist first lithographed in 1834 and painted in 1838. The Louvre picture was executed in 1838. Delacroix, from his school days to his death, was an ardent admirer of Shakespeare's genius, and was deeply impressed by the Shakesperian productions which he witnessed during his short sojourn in London.

THE CRUCIFIXION
(In the Louvre)

This small panel, which forms part of the Thomas Thiery bequest to the Louvre, is a picture of precious quality and soft colouring, painted for his friend, Mme. de Forget, who had exercised her influence in official quarters when Delacroix endeavoured to obtain the post of director of the Gobelins manufactory. It was painted in 1848. There are numerous replicas in existence.

THE BRIDE OF ABYDOS
(In the Louvre)

A great reader of English literature, Delacroix found the inspiration for many remarkable paintings in the works of Byron, who was one of the idols of the French Romanticists. As was his wont, Delacroix produced several versions of this subject, which shows Zuleika trying to prevent Selim from giving the signal to his comrades. A smaller variant, painted like the Louvre picture in 1843, and measuring only 14 in. by 10 in., realised the high price of £1282 at public auction in 1874.

DANTE AND VIRGIL
(In the Louvre)

This is the great picture with which Delacroix, then twenty-four years of age, made his debut at the Salon of 1822. The dramatic power of the central group and the frenzied movement and superb modelling of the nude figures clinging to the boat, caused an immense sensation with a public accustomed to the frigid classicism of the David School. Unfortunately the picture is now badly cracked and discoloured, probably owing to the use of bituminous pigment, which Delacroix only discarded at a later period.

THE EXECUTION OF THE DOGE MARINO FALIERO
(In the Wallace Collection)

Delacroix himself considered this picture, which was painted in 1826, to be his masterpiece. Exhibited first at the Salon of 1827, when "The Death of Sardanapalus" caused a veritable torrent of abuse to be showered upon the artist, it failed to attract the favourable attention which its nobly balanced design, brilliant colour, and intensely dramatic feeling would otherwise surely have commanded, and which was given to it in the following year by the London public. "Marino Faliero" is unquestionably the finest example of Delacroix's art in England.


FAUST AND MEPHISTOPHELES
(In the Wallace Collection)

It was probably during his visit to London in 1825 that Delacroix first realised the pictorial possibilities of Goethe's great drama. His correspondence shows that he was deeply impressed with a performance of "Faust" which he witnessed in London, and which probably suggested to him the series of nineteen lithographs, published by Sautelet in 1828. Goethe himself referred to these lithographs in terms of exaggerated praise. The catalogue of Delacroix's works includes quite a number of paintings illustrative of scenes from "Faust," of which the one in the Wallace Collection is one of the most successful.

CRESCENT MOON PUBLISHING

web: www.crmoon.com e-mail: cresmopub@yahoo.co.uk

ARTS, PAINTING, SCULPTURE

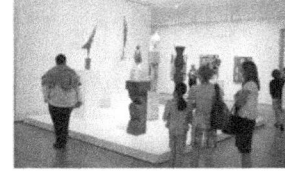
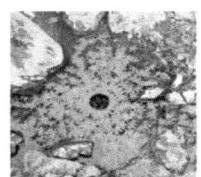
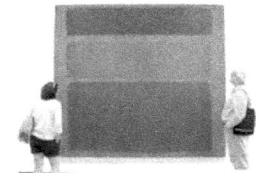

The Art of Andy Goldsworthy
Andy Goldsworthy: Touching Nature
Andy Goldsworthy in Close-Up
Andy Goldsworthy: Pocket Guide
Andy Goldsworthy In America
Land Art: A Complete Guide
The Art of Richard Long
Richard Long: Pocket Guide
Land Art In the UK
Land Art in Close-Up
Land Art In the U.S.A.
Land Art: Pocket Guide
Installation Art in Close-Up
Minimal Art and Artists In the 1960s and After
Colourfield Painting
Land Art DVD, TV documentary
Andy Goldsworthy DVD, TV documentary
The Erotic Object: Sexuality in Sculpture From Prehistory to the Present Day
Sex in Art: Pornography and Pleasure in Painting and Sculpture
Postwar Art
Sacred Gardens: The Garden in Myth, Religion and Art
Glorification: Religious Abstraction in Renaissance and 20th Century Art
Early Netherlandish Painting
Leonardo da Vinci
Piero della Francesca
Giovanni Bellini
Fra Angelico: Art and Religion in the Renaissance
Mark Rothko: The Art of Transcendence
Frank Stella: American Abstract Artist
Jasper Johns
Brice Marden
Alison Wilding: The Embrace of Sculpture
Vincent van Gogh: Visionary Landscapes
Eric Gill: Nuptials of God
Constantin Brancusi: Sculpting the Essence of Things
Max Beckmann
Caravaggio
Gustave Moreau
Egon Schiele: Sex and Death In Purple Stockings
Delizioso Fotografico Fervore: Works In Process 1
Sacro Cuore: Works In Process 2
The Light Eternal: J.M.W. Turner
The Madonna Glorified: Karen Arthurs

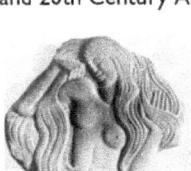
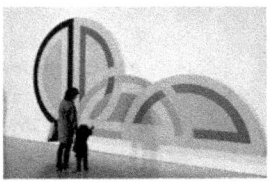
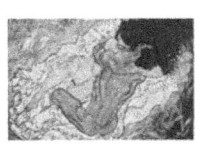
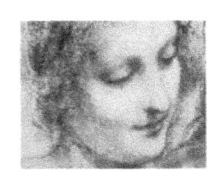
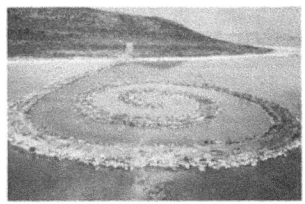

# LITERATURE

J.R.R. Tolkien: The Books, The Films, The Whole Cultural Phenomenon
J.R.R. Tolkien: Pocket Guide
Tolkien's Heroic Quest
The *Earthsea* Books of Ursula Le Guin
Beauties, Beasts and Enchantment: Classic French Fairy Tales
German Popular Stories by the Brothers Grimm
Philip Pullman and *His Dark Materials*
Sexing Hardy: Thomas Hardy and Feminism
Thomas Hardy's *Tess of the d'Urbervilles*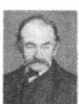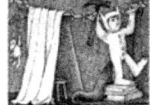
Thomas Hardy's *Jude the Obscure*
Thomas Hardy: The Tragic Novels
Love and Tragedy: Thomas Hardy
The Poetry of Landscape in Hardy
Wessex Revisited: Thomas Hardy and John Cowper Powys
Wolfgang Iser: Essays and Interviews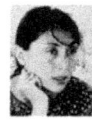
Petrarch, Dante and the Troubadours
Maurice Sendak and the Art of Children's Book Illustration
Andrea Dworkin
Cixous, Irigaray, Kristeva: The *Jouissance* of French Feminism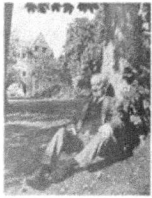
Julia Kristeva: Art, Love, Melancholy, Philosophy, Semiotics and Psychoanalysis
Hélene Cixous I Love You: The *Jouissance* of Writing
Luce Irigaray: Lips, Kissing, and the Politics of Sexual Difference
Peter Redgrove: Here Comes the Flood
Peter Redgrove: Sex-Magic-Poetry-Cornwall
Lawrence Durrell: Between Love and Death, East and West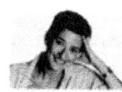
Love, Culture & Poetry: Lawrence Durrell
Cavafy: Anatomy of a Soul
German Romantic Poetry: Goethe, Novalis, Heine, Hölderlin
Feminism and Shakespeare
Shakespeare: Love, Poetry & Magic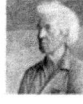
The Passion of D.H. Lawrence
D.H. Lawrence: Symbolic Landscapes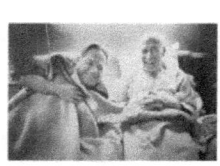
D.H. Lawrence: Infinite Sensual Violence
Rimbaud: Arthur Rimbaud and the Magic of Poetry
The Ecstasies of John Cowper Powys
Sensualism and Mythology: The Wessex Novels of John Cowper Powys
Amorous Life: John Cowper Powys and the Manifestation of Affectivity (H.W. Fawkner)
Postmodern Powys: New Essays on John Cowper Powys (Joe Boulter)
Rethinking Powys: Critical Essays on John Cowper Powys
Paul Bowles & Bernardo Bertolucci
Rainer Maria Rilke
Joseph Conrad: *Heart of Darkness*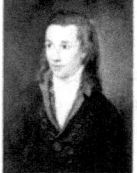
In the Dim Void: Samuel Beckett
Samuel Beckett Goes into the Silence
André Gide: Fiction and Fervour
Jackie Collins and the Blockbuster Novel
Blinded By Her Light: The Love-Poetry of Robert Graves
The Passion of Colours: Travels In Mediterranean Lands
Poetic Forms

## POETRY

Ursula Le Guin: Walking In Cornwall
Peter Redgrove: Here Comes The Flood
Peter Redgrove: Sex-Magic-Poetry-Cornwall
Dante: Selections From the Vita Nuova
Petrarch, Dante and the Troubadours
William Shakespeare: Sonnets
William Shakespeare: Complete Poems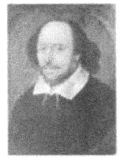
Blinded By Her Light: The Love-Poetry of Robert Graves
Emily Dickinson: Selected Poems
Emily Brontë: Poems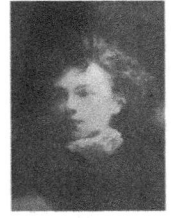
Thomas Hardy: Selected Poems
Percy Bysshe Shelley: Poems
John Keats: Selected Poems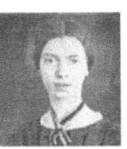
Joh n Keats: Poems of 1820
D.H. Lawrence: Selected Poems
Edmund Spenser: Poems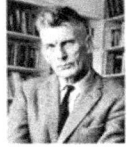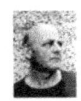
Edmund Spenser: Amoretti
John Donne: Poems
Henry Vaughan: Poems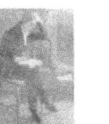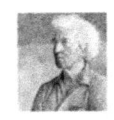
Sir Thomas Wyatt: Poems
Robert Herrick: Selected Poems
Rilke: Space, Essence and Angels in the Poetry of Rainer Maria Rilke
Rainer Maria Rilke: Selected Poems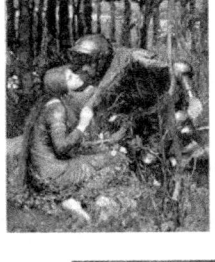
Friedrich Hölderlin: Selected Poems
Arseny Tarkovsky: Selected Poems
Arthur Rimbaud: Selected Poems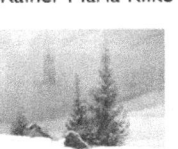
Arthur Rimbaud: A Season in Hell
Arthur Rimbaud and the Magic of Poetry
Novalis: Hymns To the Night
German Romantic Poetry
Paul Verlaine: Selected Poems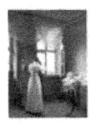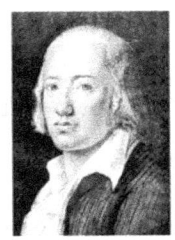
Elizaethan Sonnet Cycles
D.J. Enright: By-Blows
Jeremy Reed: Brigitte's Blue Heart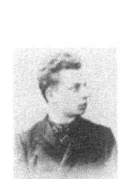
Jeremy Reed: Claudia Schiffer's Red Shoes
Gorgeous Little Orpheus
Radiance: New Poems
Crescent Moon Book of Nature Poetry
Crescent Moon Book of Love Poetry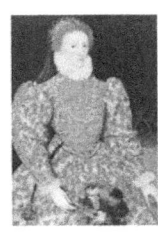
Crescent Moon Book of Mystical Poetry
Crescent Moon Book of Elizabethan Love Poetry
Crescent Moon Book of Metaphysical Poetry
Crescent Moon Book of Romantic Poetry
Pagan America: New American Poetry

MEDIA, CINEMA, FEMINISM and CULTURAL STUDIES

J.R.R. Tolkien: The Books, The Films, The Whole Cultural Phenomenon
J.R.R. Tolkien: Pocket Guide
The *Lord of the Rings* Movies: Pocket Guide
The Cinema of Hayao Miyazaki
Hayao Miyazaki: *Princess Mononoke*: Pocket Movie Guide
Hayao Miyazaki: *Spirited Away*: Pocket Movie Guide
Tim Burton : Hallowe'en For Hollywood
Ken Russell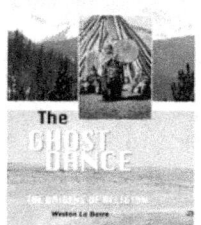
Ken Russell: *Tommy*: Pocket Movie Guide
The Ghost Dance: The Origins of Religion
The Peyote Cult
Cixous, Irigaray, Kristeva: The *Jouissance* of French Feminism
Julia Kristeva: Art, Love, Melancholy, Philosophy, Semiotics and Psychoanalysis
Luce Irigaray: Lips, Kissing, and the Politics of Sexual Difference
Hélene Cixous I Love You: The *Jouissance* of Writing
Andrea Dworkin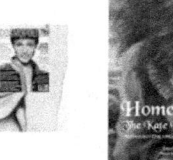
'Cosmo Woman': The World of Women's Magazines
Women in Pop Music
HomeGround: The Kate Bush Anthology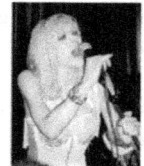
Discovering the Goddess (Geoffrey Ashe)
The Poetry of Cinema
The Sacred Cinema of Andrei Tarkovsky
Andrei Tarkovsky: Pocket Guide
Andrei Tarkovsky: *Mirror*: Pocket Movie Guide
Andrei Tarkovsky: *The Sacrifice*: Pocket Movie Guide
Walerian Borowczyk: Cinema of Erotic Dreams
Jean-Luc Godard: The Passion of Cinema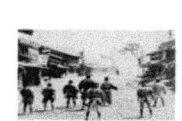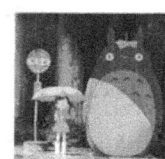
Jean-Luc Godard: *Hail Mary*: Pocket Movie Guide
Jean-Luc Godard: *Contempt*: Pocket Movie Guide
Jean-Luc Godard: *Pierrot le Fou*: Pocket Movie Guide
John Hughes and Eighties Cinema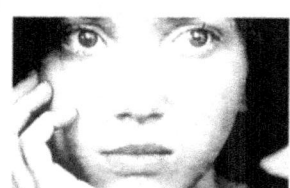
*Ferris Bueller's Day Off*: Pocket Movie Guide
Jean-Luc Godard: Pocket Guide
The Cinema of Richard Linklater
Liv Tyler: Star In Ascendance
*Blade Runner* and the Films of Philip K. Dick
Paul Bowles and Bernardo Bertolucci
Media Hell: Radio, TV and the Press
An Open Letter to the BBC
Detonation Britain: Nuclear War in the UK
Feminism and Shakespeare
Wild Zones: Pornography, Art and Feminism
Sex in Art: Pornography and Pleasure in Painting and Sculpture
Sexing Hardy: Thomas Hardy and Feminism

*The Light Eternal* is a model monograph, an exemplary job. The subject matter of the book is beautifully organised and dead on beam. (Lawrence Durrell)
It is amazing for me to see my work treated with such passion and respect. (Andrea Dworkin)

CRESCENT MOON PUBLISHING
P.O. Box 1312, Maidstone, Kent, ME14 5XU, Great Britain. www.crmoon.com

cresmopub@yahoo.co.uk   www.crescentmoon.org.uk

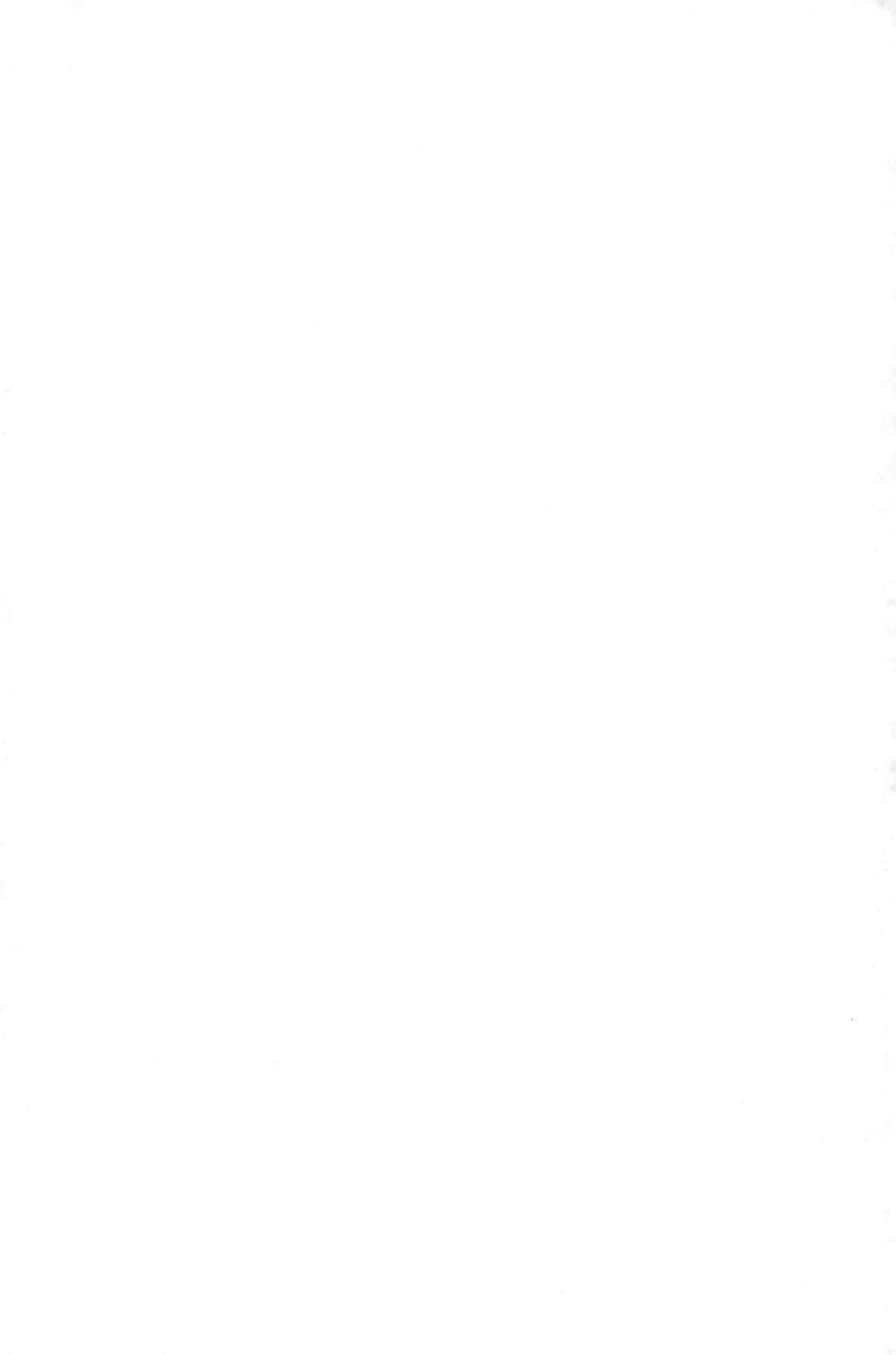